ADVANCE REVIEWS OF
Charter Schools

"As millions of parents continue seeking meaningful alternatives to traditional public schooling, enrollment in charter schools across the country in the past two decades has exploded. Waiting lists to get into good schools abound as the demand for charter schools has far outstripped their supply. Because of the newness of charters, however, books that examine or explain this important aspect of public school choice have been scarce. Even more scarce, are books written about charter schools *for parents, by parents*. Enter, Karin Piper, a parent who has chosen charter schools as the best option for her children and authored this fine book.

In *Charter Schools: The Ultimate Handbook for Parents*, Karin provides the kind of vital information that parents generally want to understand during the decision-making process about which schools are best for their children. But parents take heart! It is not written in an academic, bland tone, or full of educational psycho-bafflegab. Karin's writing style is fresh, down-to-earth, and witty. For those reasons, and because she is the first author I know to write a book for charter school parents and prospective parents, I predict that this book will be a runaway bestseller in the charter school arena. If I were a charter school leader, I would provide a free copy to every prospective family that came my way. Apart from being an inexpensive form of marketing, doing so would accomplish two worthwhile purposes: The book will help prospective families think through an important decision, and it will save schools time and money by providing information that Karin has already researched and organized.

I heartily commend this book to its readers, and Karin for her insight, perseverance, and for sharing the gift of her wit and intellect with us."

—Dr. Brian L. Carpenter
Charter School Governance & Management Consultant, Author of *Charter School Board University: An Introduction to Effective Charter School Governance* and *The Seven Outs: Strategic Planning Made Easy for Charter Schools*

"A handy guide to the basics."
—**Jay Mathews,** *Washington Post* education columnist

"A friendly resource for any reader, *Charter Schools: The Ultimate Handbook for Parents* answers questions about what charter schools are, why they exist, and how to find one that might be right for a child you know. Piper addresses issues from academic quality and charter school authorization to charter school facilities and how to be a charter school advocate."
—**Nelson Smith,** President and CEO, National Alliance for Public Charter Schools

"*Charter Schools: Kid Tested. Parent Approved. The Ultimate Handbook for Parents* educates readers about school options, demystifies the myths that surround charter schools, and presents the facts about them with clarity in this comprehensive handbook.

As a charter school parent, Ms. Piper's vast experience and knowledge of charter schools enables readers to make informed decisions about one of the most critical issues concerning their children: education. This handbook is an indispensable must for all who are responsible for making educational decisions.

With a sprinkling of humor throughout the book, the author delivers the facts in a highly informative yet enjoyable read."
—**Bernie Panitch,** Verbatim Editing

"Charter schools aren't for everyone. But we all benefit when parents are empowered with knowledge and choice. This book is a manual for all parents to take back our schools for our kids and their collective future."
—**Ben Austin,** Executive Director of Parent Revolution

"Karin simultaneously entertains, enlightens, and educates with this unique, clever look at charter schools. I've read many books about charter schools and education and I've not seen anything like *Charter Schools: The Ultimate Handbook for Parents*. If you are a parent seeking information about choices for your children's education, this is a wonderful resource. If you have children in a charter school and find yourself confused by some of the criticism of charters, this book will give you the information you need to counter the myths and misinformation. *Charter Schools* is a wonderful contribution to the worlds of education and parenting."
—**Donnell Rosenberg,** Founder of A Parents Voice in Education

"A must read for all parents and taxpayers."
—**Donna Gundle Krieg,** BlitzKrieg Publishing

"Charter Schools: Kid Tested. Parent Approved. The Ultimate Handbook for Parents, written by a true expert—a charter school parent, explains these innovative schools in laymans terms, from what they are, how they work, and what to expect as a charter school parent. There is still a lot of misinformation out there about charter schools and the author does a wonderful job at setting the record straight through her own experiences and experiences of other parents and teachers in the charter school world. Add to that a dash of humor and you truly have the *Ultimate Handbook for Parents.* This is a must read for anyone who is starting to explore public school options for their child. And for those who already have a child in a charter—the next time you are barraged with questions from friends and family about why you chose a charter school—this book will arm you with answers and provide some comic relief from another parent who has walked in your shoes. A wonderful resource!"
—**Stacy Rivera,** Director of Communications, Colorado League of Charter Schools

"An invaluable tool for any parent considering sending their child to a charter school. This guide clearly addresses parent concerns from the different types of charter schools to what to expect for homework. I found the different interviews of various students, parents, teachers and administrators particularly helpful in understanding the breadth and depth of what charter schools are all about. For example, charter school student Jordan Rowley's winning essay was both touching and insightful. It vividly illustrated how she is thriving in her charter school and how the right educational choice made all the difference in her life.

I would whole heartedly recommend this book to all prospective and current charter school families. It can help your child live up to his or her potential with its helpful and long overdue information. A brilliant resource!"   —**Sylvia Hoffmann,** New Charter School Parent

"Karin Piper's book is easy and fun to read, packed with insider information parents won't get anywhere else. Parents who are looking for alternatives to the neighborhood school should make this book their first homework assignment. "
—**Pamela Benigno,** Education Policy Director, Independence Institute

CHARTER SCHOOLS

The Ultimate Handbook for Parents

Created by

Karin Piper

Wyatt-MacKenzie Publishing, Inc.
DEADWOOD, OREGON

Charter Schools: The Ultimate Handbook for Parents
by Karin Piper

ALL RIGHTS RESERVED
©2009 by Karin Piper
ISBN: 978-1-932279-05-4
Library of Congress Control Number: 2009926788

No part of this publication may be translated, reproduced or transmitted in any form or by any means, in whole or in part, electronic or mechanical including photo-copying, recording, or by any information storage or retrieval system without prior permission in writing from the publisher.

Publisher and editor are not liable for any typographical errors, content mistakes, inaccuracies, or omissions related to the information in this book.

Product trade names or trademarks mentioned throughout this publication remain property of their respective owners.

Wyatt-MacKenzie Publishing, Inc.
DEADWOOD, OREGON

www.WyMacPublishing.com
(541) 964-3314

Requests for permission or further information should be addressed to:
Wyatt-MacKenzie Publishing, 15115 Highway 36,
Deadwood, Oregon 97430

This book is dedicated to our kids.

ABOUT THIS BOOK

Move over puffed corn. Kid testers and approving parents are no longer about cereal—they stand for school choice. The fastest-growing brand name of school choice is public charter schools. It is not just parents who favor charters. The list of approving persons also includes teachers and community leaders—even the president of the United States.

What are charter schools? Are they expensive? Should I consider a charter school for my child?

Charter Schools: The Ultimate Handbook for Parents will guide you through these commonly asked questions and more. Should you prefer technical, thesis-style material on education reform and its laws, you do have a lot of literary options. This would not be one of them.

Another word for *alternative* is *choice*, which is a word much debated when it comes to education. Who makes decisions for your child's education? Who should be responsible for such determinations? Most people have an opinion about this, and as the author of *Charter Schools: The Ultimate Handbook for Parents*, I will give you mine.

I do not claim to be the ultimate charter school parent, but this book will tell you about them. In fact, I could not have written this book without a posse of ultimate charter school parents in my ear.

You will also learn the real definition of charter schools and truths about tuition, enrollment "creaming," teacher qualifications—and more!

Charter Schools: The Ultimate Handbook for Parents is designed to provide basic information about charter schools in the United States. As the author of this book, my view and support for such schools will be clearly heard. However, the intention is not to convince you to run out and register your kids in the nearest charter school. The objective is to educate the general public about charter schools and straighten out some interesting and humorous myths along the way.

Thank you for taking the time to learn about charter schools and how they contribute to public education!

The Ultimate Handbook for Parents

Contents at a Glance

About the Author	8
Foreword	10
Acknowledgements	13
The Importance of School Choice	16
The Charter School Choice	17
Quick Facts	23

Part 1: The ABCs of Charter Schools 25
   1. What Is a Charter School? 26
      Definition and explanation
   2. The History of Charter Schools 28
      The genesis of charter schools and the creation of charter laws
   3. Why Do Parents Choose Charter Schools? 30
      Parent testimonials

Part 2: We, the People 35
   4. The Leadership 36
      Governing, directing, and producing—the complete screen credits
   5. Teachers and Staff 45
      Who teaches? Are charter school teachers qualified?
   6. The Students 58
      Are charter schools just for the troubled and the elite?
   7. The Parents 65
      Charter School Parents—the good, the bad, and the supermoms
   8. The Community 72
      *The view of charter schools from the other side of
      the neighborhood fence*

Part 3: Expectations 75
   9. The Workload 76
      Will my child be challenged or have trouble keeping up?
   10. Curricula 83
      What is the curriculum for charter schools?
   11. Character Development 92
      What is character education and why is it in the classroom?
   12. Homework 95
      What is expected on the home front?
   13. ESL, GT, and SPED 98
      Do charter schools accept special-needs students?

14. Discipline. 112
   Laying down the law at school
15. Dress Code 114
   Uniforms and dress codes
16. School Facility. 116
   What do you mean we're in trailers? And other potential building surprises
17. Transportation 120
   James, home please! Your car pool arrangements

Part 4: Choosing a Charter School 122
18. Is a Charter School Right for Your Family?. 123
   Questions you should ask yourself before charter school enrollment
19. Charter School Variety. 126
   Traditional, open classroom, online—exploring charter differences
20. Research Guide 130
   Which school is the best fit for your family? School comparison worksheets
21. Charter School Enrollment 141
   Is there a charter school litmus test? Lottery, waiting lists, first-come-first-served, and other variances

Part 5: The Charter School Life—Now That You Are a Charter School Family 145
22. Volunteering 146
   How much, how often, and what do I do when I volunteer for my charter school?
23. Teamwork 151
   The teacher-parent-student relationship
24. Outreach and Networking 160
   Connecting beyond your charter school

Part 6: Behind the Scenes 167
25. The Creation 168
   Who can start a charter school? What is a charter school authorizer?
26. Funding 179
   Show me the money. Who pays for charter school education?
27. Accountability 182
   To whom do charter schools answer and why? What is a SAC?

Part 7: And There Is More… 185
   28. My State and Charter School Law 186
      Does your state have charter school laws?
      What you can do to impact charter school legislation
   29. The Neutral Charter Schools 192
      Why charter schools are politically unbiased
   30. Lingo 199
      Creaming, handpicking, and other odd terms
   31. Starting a New Charter School 206
      Is your school district in need of a new public school option?
      Stories and advice from real people that started charter schools
   32. When Charter Schools Fail 215
      Addressing unsuccessful ventures: Why some charters don't make it,
      how often does it happen, and what do we do now?
   33. When Charter Schools Succeed 222
      The wonder of alternative public education done well
      The marvelous sensation of schools that work

Part 8: Post Script
   31 Flavors of Public Education 224
   Glossary 226
   Helpful Links 231
   Charter School Organizations 232
   Award-winning Charter Schools Index 245
   Index 251

ABOUT THE AUTHOR

My name is Karin Piper, and I am a stay at home mom in beautiful Colorado. Okay, technically I am never home, and I am more of a stay-in-the-car mom as my life consists mostly of running errands and transporting my three little angels from one place to another. That's not a complaint; it's just the top of my résumé. I don't know of anything I'd rather be than a mom. I did not choose the mothering business for a hefty salary but for the perks. What other job permits you to be around for scraped knees, and "look-what-I-can-do's," while still receiving copious praise on employee appreciation day (Mother's Day)?

While raising my children I have written for several publications including *Your Hub* (*Denver Post*), *Schools of Tomorrow* (*EdNews Colorado*), the *Examiner* (Colorado Charter School Examiner), and more. My favorite piece was probably "It Mattress to Me," an article about a weird photo with two campaign signs on a filthy mattress in the suburbs. It was featured as "Best of 2008" in the *Denver Post's* Your Hub Blog section for Parker, Colorado.

Along with being a mother and a writer, I am also a volunteer and an advocate for our schools and public libraries. It has been my good fortune to be able to work with wonderful organizations such as the Douglas County Libraries, the Colorado League of Charter Schools, and a collection of area schools.

I was born and raised in Sweden and landed in the United States through a student exchange program. During that year I learned a whole lot of English, a new culture, and how to fall in love with an American boy. The latter was not difficult at all. It is now more than twenty years since I fell in love with my American man and it is he who is my great supportive husband and the father of my three children.

Our family car pool has been heading toward a local charter school since the beginning of this millennium (2002). I must say I didn't know much about charter schools, what they are, and what makes them unique. I was just incredibly thankful that our public school district offered a solution for our son's academic needs. Throughout the years, it is not just my children who have been learning, but I have gained knowledge as well. By discovering charter schools through personal experience, I consider myself "street smart" on the topic. My personal journey of evolving into an informed, "school-choice parent" is paved with tales of confusion, frustration, hilarity, and the unbeatable spirit of community partnership. Becoming a charter school parent no longer needs to be learned the hard way. Connect with parents who walk in chartered shoes, read, consult the Internet, and visit charter schools. Even if you decide charter schools are not your cup of java, you will become one savvy parent who is equipped to make a great school choice for your child.

That's an awful lot of talk about me, and I would rather hear about you. You can contact me through my Web site at www.charterschoolmom.com.

FOREWORD

Educating the students in our public schools has never been more rewarding or challenging. This is especially true of all the hundreds of charter schools that have opened. Helen Keller once stated: "One can never consent to creep when one feels an impulse to soar." When it comes to charter schools, that statement catches the vision of founders and parents who have decided to engage in the excitement of creating or having their children attend such a school.

Having started three charter schools in the Colorado Springs area, I can tell you there are many hurdles to overcome but also much satisfaction when you see the type of education the students are receiving. All three schools, Cheyenne Mountain Charter Academy, James Irwin Charter High School and Colorado Springs Early Colleges, address specific needs that were unmet by the traditional public schools. Their lasting success pays tribute to the mission and vision created for students by these schools.

The ability to create new schools provides a unique opportunity to start something entrepreneurial in a highly managed public school system. It is my firm belief that charter schools have helped all of us work to accomplish higher academic achievement for all students, whether or not they attend a charter school.

This book takes a comprehensive look at charter schools and provides information in a light and friendly way that excites you to read the whole book. Karin Piper has done a great job in writing it. It is my hope that it will encourage more entrepreneurs to start a charter school and parents to put their students in one. The free market of ideas is alive and well in this country. This book will truly help some of you soar to the challenge. After all, it is people who are the greatest resource of this country. God Speed in your journey.

Senator Keith King
COLORADO SENATE, Education Committee

ACKNOWLEDGMENTS

Thank God!

I don't mean that in a blasphemous sense, but in sincere gratitude to our creator.

There have been times in the past several months when I was not sure how and why pieces of this project came together. All I can say is that without the good Lord, this manuscript would still be idling on page one. There were many days when writing began and ended on a prayer.

Many of these prayers were about connecting with really smart charter school experts to provide answers and resources.

Let's face it; I'm *just* a charter school mom. Without a posse of incredible individuals and organizations, none of this would ever have been written. These are the people behind the scenes who make our public charter schools possible to begin with. Let me start from the beginning.

Thanks to the entire staff at the Colorado League of Charter Schools (CLCS). You guys have no idea what Jim Griffin, Sean Bradley, and especially Stacy Rivera have had to endure while this book had been in progress. It is a miracle that these guys still answer their phones. Every time that phone rang, they risked being peppered with a round of questions from one of the charter school parents in Colorado. Stacy has also connected me with several individuals, and without them the project would not have lifted off the ground. If it wasn't for Stacy and CLCS, I probably wouldn't have kept writing about charter schools for very long, as I would have run out of information.

Susie Miller Barker at the National Association of Charter School Authorizers, Todd Ziebarth at the National Alliance for Public Charter Schools, Jonathan Oglesby at the Center for Education Reform, and Pam Benigno from the Independence Institute are a few of these key supporters. When it comes to charter schools from a national perspective, these are the go-to folks.

Donnell Rosenberg (*A Parent's Voice*) has become a dear friend, and operated much as a voice of sanity. Donnell also has a much more defined view of politics than what I do, and she has helped me tremendously with understanding some of the issues surrounding our local charter schools. She is unafraid of speaking her mind, and one of the strongest advocates for parental rights to choice in education that I've ever known.

Then we have the scores of charter school leaders, founders, teachers, directors, students, and parents who submitted information and stories about their charter school experiences. In addition to the many charter schools that are featured throughout the book, there is a list of more than seventy award-winning schools in the index of this book!

Nancy Cleary of Wyatt-MacKenzie Publishing deserves an honorable mention for taking a chance on an unusual topic with an unknown author.

Last, but not least, my family deserves a huge thank you.

My husband, Jeff Piper, the love of my life and the wind beneath my wings, is an absolute saint. If you don't agree with me now, you will soon, as my offbeat sense of humor is in print throughout this entire book. Every time you roll your eyes at one of my bad jokes, think about what my husband endures on a daily basis.

And to my kids, who have taken me on this journey. If it wasn't for them—well, I wouldn't be sitting here writing this book, because I would not be a *charter school mom*.

A grand thank you to all!

DISCLAIMER

This book is designed to provide information on charter schools. It is sold with the understanding that the publisher and the author are not engaged in rendering legal or other professional services. If legal or other expert advice is required, the services of a competent professional should be sought.

It is not the purpose of this manual to reprint all the information that is otherwise available to parents, educators, and business professionals, but instead to complement, amplify, and supplement other texts.

You are urged to read all the available material, learn as much as possible about school options, and tailor the information to your individual needs. For more information, see the many resources in the appendix.

Charter schools, like any school, are not a one-size-fits-all solution. People who pursues a charter school as a chosen form of education must expect to invest a lot of time and effort in their child's schooling success. For many families, charter schools have served as solid public school options that meet the unique needs of their individual students.

Every effort has been made to make this handbook as complete and accurate as possible. However, there may be mistakes, both typographical and in content. Therefore, this text should only be used as a general guide and not the ultimate source of charter school information. Furthermore, this manual contains information on charter schools that is current only up to the printing date.

The purpose of this manual is to entertain and educate. The author and publisher shall have neither liability nor responsibility to any person or entity with respect to any loss or damage caused, or alleged to have been caused, directly or indirectly, by the information contained in this book.

If you do not wish to be bound by the above, you may return this book to the publisher according to the publisher refund policy.

The Importance of School Choice

Who makes choices for your child? If you asked my kids this question they'd tell you they do. Don't let them fool you. If this were the case, they'd run around dirty, eat nothing but crap, and stay up until the cows came home. The person who does the choosing is responsible for the results of decisions made—the good, bad, and indifferent. If you don't believe me, imagine feeding your kid a heap of sugar and then sending them to the neighbors for an afternoon. Don't try this at home—not even in your mother-in-law's home.

Clearly choices come with consequences, some more permanent than others. Education definitely falls within the category of potential, long-term side effects. Parents decide what is best for their kids. After all, as parents we are also the ones accountable for future consequences. So why is it that some folks feel that the government knows best about what type of school is a proper fit for your kid? Is it that the state knows your kid better than you, the parent? Or is it that the government wants to be responsible for the consequences?

The irony is that it is generally the people that advise government-knows-best-education that wag a finger at "uninvolved parents" when reports of failing schools come out. On the flip side, the government has a place in our public schools since they are funded with public taxpayer dollars. But choosing the school that is the best fit for your child still belongs to the parent.

I am a believer that parent involvement in education makes the difference between failure and success. However, the parents should be enabled to make educational decisions for their children from the get-go. A child should not need to endure educational failure before it's acceptable for a parent to represent their student's needs.

Regardless of the school you pick, you are making a choice. Placing your child in a neighborhood public school is a choice, too! Quality education is a children's right issue. Selecting which education better fits the child is a matter of parental rights.

The Charter School Choice

There is a vast ocean of school choices including homeschooling, private, online, and magnet schools. How do charter schools contribute to the education assortment?

Charter schools are affordable to all families

Prior to charter school law school choice was for the rich. Private school tuition and homeschooling may be impossible for a low-income family. Since charter schools are public schools there are no tuition fees; hence, they are viable alternatives for families regardless of background and income.

Charter schools provide education diversity within public schools

States with charter school laws have created fantastic opportunities for school districts to serve their students with diverse needs, hence retaining more students who may otherwise need to seek options beyond public education. Progressive public schools have strong partnerships with their charter school counterparts and work collaboratively and inclusively to effectively meet the needs of its students.

This is the type of relationship we will see more of as state lawmakers and education leaders increasingly gain awareness of the advantages of public charter schools.

Charter schools offer innovative teaching methods

Since charters have fewer regulations than other public schools, they can explore cutting-edge teaching tools and curricula that may take longer for other schools to implement.

The benefit is on several levels: firstly, the charter school teachers and students may experience immediate gains; secondly, the greater public school system would have the advantage of having another educational entity implement new programs.

If you question the benefit of this, ask yourself how you feel about anything that is "version one"; let it be a car, computer, or service. Version one is notorious for recalls and updates. It is an advantage for traditional schools to observe other public schools trying out a new program or service to learn what worked and what didn't.

A friend of mine bought a new cell phone that I had been drooling over for some time. It was a well advertised little number, which had all the bells and whistles. It was also a new release. Although I don't wish my friends to go through difficulty (not even with something as trivial as a cell phone), I must say I learned tons about that snazzy phone through her imperfect experience.

Charter Schools are designed with specific criteria

Charter school agreements are written with specific purposes. There are charter schools that cater to gifted and talented students, at-risk youth (a term used loosely as all kids who do not get their educational needs met are at risk of not graduating), pregnant teens, and many more. Charter schools are like snowflakes; they are unique, even compared with one another.

Charter schools drive up the overall quality of education

This is a topic I cover carefully. Some feel that charter schools are competition to other public schools; I do not agree. Charter schools provide educational options unique from traditional schools. Many of these charter students would end up in a private or homeschooling situation should their current charter education cease to exist.

Education is not a commodity product; hence it does not compete. If you think about it, you cannot apply the "supply and demand" principle to education. Demand for good education does not go up and down. It is a constant. The number of students may vary, but the demand for quality education does not change. Supply of excellent education may unfortunately vary, but due to different circumstances than demand.

However, where there is choice, quality goes up. When students are not held hostage by schooling of default, education leaders pay extra attention. If quality is not maintained, the students have the choice to be serviced elsewhere.

Although comparing charter school offerings with its traditional peers is like comparing apples and oranges, it is still fruit. If the apples are rotten, there may be a rush for oranges and vice versa. The fruit vendor is prudent to assure his offering is top notch when there is a choice.

Here is a terrific article written by Alexander Ooms (who serves on the board of West Denver Preparatory Charter Schools), which describes the difference between choice and competition.

Competition vs. Choice
By Alexander Ooms

Denver Public Schools' recent decision to have different schools share buildings provoked fearful cries of "increased competition" among some neighborhood advocates. But these objections blur the important distinction between competition and choice.

While unfettered competition could well have a negative impact on public education, managed choice (and the resulting academic specialization) can benefit everyone.

Organizations that offer commodity products compete primarily on price (think gas stations). Those that offer non-commodities compete by having different products or services. Public education is not a commodity product, but defenders of the status quo often act like it is, and assume that adding a second school to a half-full building can only mean the demise of the original school.

That assumption is unfounded. Demand for commodity products does not increase with more choice (i.e., one does not buy more gas because there are two stations). But demand often increases for products that are reasonably distinct, even if they are located right next door.

If, within a single building, one gives different schools the autonomy and ability to better focus their academic programs, there is no reason to think they won't both attract more students and do a better job helping them learn.

The common example of this differentiation in business is Starbucks, which took an industry with a single bland offering and both introduced new products (skinny caramel soy latte, anyone?) and provided better service. Surprisingly, instead of a new Starbucks resulting in the demise of all nearby coffee shops as once feared, it often helps them. According to the Specialty Coffee Association of America, from 2000 to 2005, in the midst of Starbucks' period of rapid growth, the number of independent coffeehouses grew 40%.

This phenomenon is not limited to business. There is a large body of research on the tendency of like-minded organizations to "cluster" and the benefits that clustering brings. In industries as varied as textiles, medical research and the visual arts, similar organizations in close proximity see increases in both innovation and productivity.

Of course, public education is not coffee. Opening a public school requires significant planning and a lengthy application process carefully vetted by both DPS and the Board of Education with considerable community input. Any competition is carefully weighed among different factions, and Colorado's school choice law ensures that there is no centralized planning such that students are required to attend a specific school. Increasingly, the role of public school boards includes the approval and oversight of new schools, a process DPS manages increasingly well.

What DPS has achieved through the decision to share school buildings is the ability to offer students and families carefully placed educational choices that can help all schools, placing programs together that often complement each other or allow each to focus on their strengths. Thus, West High School will share with Edison, a middle school that could easily increase the number and academic preparation of kids eventually attending West. Kunsmiller Creative Arts Academy, slated as a K-12 integrated arts school, will share a facility with sixth- to eighth-grade West Denver Prep, which overlaps in middle school years but will offer a different, highly structured curriculum and culture.

Smiley Middle School, with a specific International Baccalaureate program, will share with a new Envision school that features project-based learning. An elementary school run by the Denver teachers union will share with a high school expansion from the nationally successful Knowledge is Power Program.

Managed choice is important because there is no single school model that works for all kids. Increasingly, the idea of a single school that is the right fit for every child in a neighborhood is problematic. No one disputes that kids can be vastly different, so why do we demand that different kids attend only one local school?

Having different schools in close proximity allows each the option to specialize. New York City recently graded its public schools, and the eight specialized schools within the city all received the highest ranking. It is likewise no coincidence that the two best high schools in DPS—located less than a mile apart—are both highly focused: Denver School of the Arts and Denver School of Science and Technology.

When opponents decry "competition" in shared buildings, they overlook the benefits: Increased and better school choices will help more of Denver's families choose some form of public education in one of its evolving flavors. And the truth is that competition for public schools already exists in private schools or in dropping out altogether. This is the competition that public school advocates should fear most—not the choice of a different educational program in the same building.

Quick Facts

This Q & A will cover the ten most commonly asked charter school questions. Detailed information on each topic will be covered throughout the book.

1. What is a charter school?

A charter school is a public school that is operated by an entity other than its district (or authorizer) and accountable for its student's performance. *See chapter 1.*

2. Are charter schools public or private schools?

Charter schools are ***public schools***. *See chapter 1.*

3. Do charter schools charge tuition?

No. *See chapter 1.*

4. How are charter schools different than traditional schools?

Charters are designed to be autonomous from their district (or authorizer) and answer to fewer regulations than its traditional counterpart, but are held accountable for student achievement. *See chapter 1.*

5. How is a charter school funded?

Charter schools receive state funding, and in some cases federal, grant, and local tax revenue shares. *See chapter 26.*

6. Do charter schools handpick their students?

No. Charter schools are public schools and must follow antidiscrimination laws. *See chapters 21 and 30.*

7. Are charter school teachers qualified?

Yes. *See chapter 5.*

8. Do charter school students take standardized tests?

Yes.

9. Does my state have charter school laws?

Forty states and the District of Columbia and Puerto Rico have signed charter school law as of May2009.

See chapter 28 and the appendix.

10. Is a charter school right for my family?

Only you can decide this. *Charter Schools: The Ultimate Handbook for Parents* will provide you with basic information and worksheets for your research. *See chapters 18, 19, 20, and 21.*

Part 1

The ABCs of Charter Schools

In Part 1:

1. What Is a Charter School?
   Definition and explanation for parents
2. The History of Charter Schools
   The genesis of charter schools and the creation of charter laws
3. Why Do Parents Choose Charter Schools?
   Parent testimonials

OVERVIEW

- What is a "charter school?"

- The definition of a charter school and the purpose they serve is one of the misinterpreted topics of education today.

- Part 1 will provide parents with the basic facts on charter school origins.

- You will also get that nagging question answered: why do parents choose charter schools?

- The answers will come directly from charter school parents.

- This is the beginning of your education about charter schools.

CHAPTER 1
What Is a Charter School?

Definitions of Charter Schools:

"Charter schools are nonsectarian public schools of choice that operate with freedom from many of the regulations that apply to traditional public schools." —*US Charter Schools*

"Charter schools are semiautonomous public schools, founded by educators, parents, community groups, or private organizations that operate under a written contract with a state, district, or other entity." —*Education Committee of the States*

"The term 'charter school' means a public school that: in accordance with a specific State statute authorizing the granting of charters to schools, is exempt from significant state or local rules that inhibit the flexible operation and management of public schools, but not from any rules relating to the other requirements of this paragraph [the paragraph that sets forth the Federal definition]." —*U.S. Department of Education, No Child Left behind, Charter Schools Program*

Charter School [noun];

Charter schools are innovative and independent public schools run by an entity other than its authorizer. These schools are produced by parents, organizations, or community groups to fill an educational need not otherwise offered by traditional schools.

There are two principles that guide charter schools: they are operationally autonomous public schools, exempt from many of the procedural requirements of district public schools, and they are accountable for student achievement.

Charter schools are intended to be unique of its traditional public school counterpart. That's just the whole point—isn't it? If offering a public school option, creating more of the same would simply defy the purpose. Why bother with education reform if it is not with the goal of improving the offering that already exists?

There is no magic bullet, and there is no "one-size-fits all" education. What works beautifully for one student is a disaster for another. Our traditional public schools are set up to offer education for the general masses. In some cases it works, other times not so much.

The reason a child is not learning to his or her full potential is not always the fault of poor national education or an inferior teacher. Sometimes a student just falls outside the peripheral lines of his or her learning environment. Whether your child is bored out of his gourd and needs more of a challenge, or falling behind the rest of the class, finding a solution is pertinent. Ignoring a child's individual education needs can evolve into a future disaster.

So what is a parent to do for a child that fits this description? First, you (the parent) are your child's advocate. Without your involvement and support little can be done to improve the situation. Second, you need to consult a professional who can advise about your child's specific requirements. Your school district or state education department can provide you with contact information to such specialists in your area.

Contact information for your state's education department is in the appendix of *Charter Schools: The Ultimate Handbook for Parents.* Next, it is time to research your education options, and that's what you are doing by reading this book. We will give you the tools to do this in future chapters, but before you start working the formulas, we recommend that you read the preceding chapters.

Making a school choice is a tough decision and research should always begin with understanding the principles behind each option.

Do not choose a school based on anybody else's opinion but your own.

The above sentence, my friend, is the fine print of this book.

CHAPTER 2

The History of Charter Schools

Once upon a time in 1974, there were no charter schools. Along came a professor named Ray Budde. He was one of those kind-looking fellows with the same hairdo as Mr. Clean. Budde was a teacher and an enthusiast of organizational theories. He channeled both these passions into a paper for the Society for General Systems and titled it "Education by Charter." The response to this paper was as anticlimactic as it was unanimous—there was none.

Apparently Budde's colleagues did not feel that there was much of a problem with the existing structure of the educational system. So Budde stashed his solution to a nonexistent problem away for a decade or so. Thank goodness that paper shredders were not all the rage yet.

Then the 1980s came along. The United States was moonwalking in parachute pants and entertained by *The Breakfast Club* and *Saved by the Bell*. We also received *The Nation at Risk* and the *Carnegie Forum* reports. Suddenly, through the ozone-thinning cloud of Aqua Net hairspray, it became clear: There was a problem with our schools. Our educational system needed a face-lift.

Budde dug out his old paper and managed to get it published by the *Northeast Regional Lab*. He also did what every self-respecting, recently published author would do—and mailed a copy to the serving president of the United States—George H.W. Bush.

Then one Sunday in July, Mrs. Budde noted that her hubby had made the paper. She pointed to a column that reported the *American Federation of Teachers*' support of the notion of having teachers initiate autonomous schools. The AFT president, Albert Shanker, was even quoted stating that Budde had the best name for these schools: "charter schools."

The AFT teachers union was already one of the most organized sectors in the country, much to Shanker's credit. Shanker, like Budde, was a teacher at heart. He had built a career upon opposing unfairness toward teachers—low pay and lack of voice. Shanker's early support of charter schools really should not be such a surprise. He was famous for challenging his union members on its priorities, and being crystal clear that serving members meant serving the students and the public. It is noteworthy, however, that he was not a cheerleader for school choice.

Budde's paper, "Education by Charter," was a proposal of school district restructuring. It suggested the district should change from a "four-level line and staff organization," to a "two- level in which groups of teachers would receive educational charters directly from the school board." The chartering groups of teachers would be held responsible for the instruction. Some called this the "contract district." The Education Commission of the States (ECS) dubbed it the "all-charter district."

Budde's "Education by Charter" was directed at existing schools. But his new pal, Al Shanker, suggested charter schools would be new schools in their own buildings. It was not long until this concept was brought to legislation. Minnesota was the first state to embrace charter schools as reform. It took a few attempts to get the law to fly, but fly it did. Minnesota Governor Arne Carlson signed the first charter school law into effect in 1991. In 1994, with strong support of the Clinton administration, that legislation was adopted and encouraged the rest of the states to pass and implement it.

There is irony in the fact that charter schools were propelled by a union man like Al Shanker, since they are traditionally unaffiliated with the teachers' unions. Shanker was really not pleased with this and officially expressed his dismay with the movement. Ray Budde said charter schools looked different than what he had originally envisioned, but he was pleased. Thankfully we know enough about charter schools and their success today to have a diverse group of supporters from all sides of the political podium.

Ray Budde died of respiratory failure, having suffered from lung cancer, on June 11, 2005. Al Shanker passed away from bladder cancer in 1997. President Bill Clinton awarded Shanker the *Presidential Medal of Freedom*, posthumously in 1998.

The rest, as they say, is history.

Does your state have charter school laws? More on this in chapter 28. You may also refer to the appendix at any time to look up resources for your state's department of education.

CHAPTER 3

Why Do Parents Choose Charter Schools?

Suppose the question really is why parents actively pursue school options in general.

To date, I have never been told that someone selected a charter school simply because it's governed a certain way, or that it was cheaper for the taxpayer. No, the recurring answer to why parents seek education alternatives is because it offers something unique for their child.

The following comments are what some parents say their charter schools offer their children and why it is a good choice for them (some letters were edited for length):

"Dear Reader,

I have two kids, Hilary and Micaela, at Toledo School of the Arts (TSA). Both of them are sweet, bright, talented, solid 'A' students who came to TSA after *languishing* in the private, public, and parochial systems.

Other schools offered our girls little more than rote classroom learning. And while they learned classroom material just fine, I know their individualism suffered. Busywork, regimentation, and pressure to conform in the classroom translated on a social level to cliques, social status, peer pressure, and exclusivity.

I don't see much evidence of any of that at TSA. There are a lot of 'different' students at TSA whose individual quirks, appearance, talents, and personalities are embraced. Whereas many of these kids would be—or in fact, *were* —bullied at other schools, the environment and culture at TSA is one of acceptance. I can't begin to describe how important this is in bringing out the amazing, hidden talents and aspirations these kids have inside them. It is to the great benefit of our society that we continue to allow and encourage them to express themselves. It is easy to see what a positive effect it has had on my kids—academically, socially, and emotionally—to be affirmed, encouraged, and valued for their individuality and unique talents. They are happy!

By any objective measure, TSA provides an academic experience on a par with any school in Northwest Ohio. The energy of the school, the enthusiasm of the students *and staff,* create an environment that fosters intuitive learning and long-term retention. But that is not all there is to education. TSA 'gets' the human aspect of education.

Notwithstanding they are a little older now, I don't worry so much about how my girls will get by as adults. They are more purposeful after a couple of years at TSA. I get the sense that their inner compass is stronger than ever and that they know who they are and where they are going. And I believe that TSA deserves a great deal of credit for that.

I am passionate in my support of this school. In all my experience with education—my children's as well as my own (all the way through graduate and medical school)—I have *never* said about any school what I reserve for TSA and what I have said to many people: **I *love* this school!"**

—*Joseph A. Tore, MD, MBA, parent at Toledo School of the Arts (OH)*

"I was fortunate to stumble upon a wonderful school option for my children.

We were chosen in the lottery at a charter school after we had already completed all the paperwork for my oldest son to attend kindergarten in the neighborhood school. But we had *won!* So the charter school was where he would begin kindergarten.

Seven years later, he is still in the same school, now along with his younger brother.

I am a parent who did not do a lot of research before my son started school. These years have been a journey of discovery for me, as well as for my children. I think I grow more grateful each day, as I realize what a perfect fit it has been all along; I realize how different my children's fate might have been had it not been for the *luck of the draw*. The school provides a small, safe, caring culture with a rigorous curriculum. My boys are being very well prepared for their high school education and beyond.

My charter school teaches the Core Knowledge sequence. I am continually amazed by the exciting facts they are learning in science, geography, history, and literature. I wish I had enjoyed such a rich education as a child.

All children are different, including my two sons. My older one has always been in advanced classes. My younger one struggled to learn to read. His teachers and reading specialists developed a learning plan to fit his needs. They followed him closely and always communicated with me about how we could help and support his progress at home. This boy started first grade well behind most of his classmates. He is now in third grade and has caught up to most of his classmates (surpassing several); his confidence has grown incredibly.

Charter schools are self-governed. By attending monthly governing board meetings I have access to the decision making process in our school. The heavy parental involvement produces strong, direct accountability. My charter school is a community of caring adults, staff, and parents who want to see the students grow and thrive. My involvement there is needed and encouraged.

There are hundreds and hundreds of children on waiting lists for the charter schools in my school district. In addition to being a volunteer in my children's school, I advocate on behalf of charter schools and parental choice in education. I want all parents to have the right they deserve to choose the best educational option for their children."

—*Donnell Rosenberg, charter school parent and founder of A Parents Voice, a grassroots school-choice organization.*

"Dear Reader,

I choose a charter school because my five-year-old was reading at a second-grade level.

The private school where he attended preschool informed us that he wouldn't be a good fit at the school because they didn't have any way to challenge him. The local school was at the time reported to have trouble with drug dealers nearby campus. We did *not* view that environment as a sound option.

Cole Academy (then Michigan Early Elementary Center) is a K-5 program and was the first Charter School in Lansing, MI. It had operated as a private school for twenty-five years before it became a charter and had an outstanding reputation. They had two teachers and a para-professional in each classroom. Students were grouped by ability, and worked in small math or reading groups of two to six students with one teacher.

Michael was in the five-year-old room for almost two weeks before he was moved to the five- to six-year-old room. He did second grade math and reading as a kindergartener, and advanced a year or two in math or reading abilities each year.

After fifth grade Michael enrolled in Windermere Park Charter Academy. His placement test showed that he was currently at a ninth-grade level in math. At the time new sixth graders were not permitted to advance in math (this policy later changed). Michael told me constantly that he wasn't learning anything new in math, a frustration that I communicated with the school.

There wasn't a fast or easy fix.

By seventh grade a math teacher came up with a plan. He challenged Michael at his skill level and recruited him as an after-school 'peer math tutor.'

In eighth grade, the charter school was able to offer Michael even more. Michael was still enrolled in Windermere Park Charter Academy and took the majority of courses there, but he was learning math at Michigan State University's CHAMPS (Cooperative Highly Accelerated Math Program). At the year's end Michael had finished two years of high school math.

The charter school recognized Michael's unique needs and paid for his participation in CHAMPS.

Charter schools give great options to parents.

In Lansing, charters have improved the local public schools, which now offer magnet programs. Education is no longer a monopoly. Schools must compete for students and state dollars. In any school, parents need to be an advocate for their child. Get to know the principal and staff, so your child can have the quality education they deserve."

—*Mary Harding, a parent speaking about Windermere Park Charter Academy, (MI)*

"Hello,

My name is Suzanne Bolden. I am a parent of a second grader who is enrolled in James Irwin Charter Elementary School (JICS). He came from a school where we felt he was treated unfairly.

Before searching for another school, I gave chance after chance (to his past school) to see a change in the behavior of my son; he wasn't succeeding in any area but art, which just isn't acceptable. When he started at JICS, it was a struggle the first year. His grades and attitude did get better, but I expected better academic results. This year, he is above average, passing with all As and one B. We are very proud of his hard work and pleased with all staff that comes in contact with him.

I am very pleased with the expectations from the students and teachers and everyone who is held accountable and responsible for their actions as a whole and individuals. The curriculum can sometimes seem somewhat hard, but I do believe it is building character in the students and promotes success at the school. It makes the students and family members of the students very proud of the final results.

All the staff is excellent with the students, and the communication with the parents is outstanding. In some public schools, it just seems the teachers didn't care about the students and whether they fail or succeed, and sometimes that can't be helped due to the ratio and the curriculum that is being used.

I am so excited about my second child starting kindergarten (at JICS) in 2009. I have and will continue to refer JICS to other parents."

—*Suzanne Bolden, parent at James Irwin Charter Elementary School (CO)*

Part 2

We, the People

In Part 2:

4. The Leadership
    Governing, directing, and producing—the complete screen credits
5. Teachers and Staff
    Who hires, fires, and teaches? Are charter school teachers qualified?
6. The Students
    Are charter schools for the troubled or for the elite?
7. The Parents
    Charter School Parents—the good, bad, and the supermoms
8. The Community
    The view of charter schools from the other side of the neighborhood fence

Family should be like cheesecake—sweet, rich, and in small portions.

Although such hopes rarely come to fruition, it's your family and you love them. Sometimes they drive you nuts. But if someone criticizes them unfairly, you will be the first to come to their defense.

If your kids are enrolled in a charter school, the staff, teachers, parents, and leaders become your school family. You will learn to value them for who they are. But mostly you will come to appreciate them for how they contribute to your child's education.

After all, who doesn't have room in their lives for a little cheesecake?

OVERVIEW

- Part 2 will cover the basic family tree of a charter school.

- We will also answer questions such as "Are charter school teachers qualified?" "Who attends a charter school?" and "Who's the boss?"

CHAPTER 4

The Leadership

What did the eraser say to the pencil? Take me to your ruler.

I continue to impress with sophisticated humor.

By now you have had a few facts imprinted on your brain. One is "Charter schools are public schools which operate independently of their authorizer."

That clearly begs for the follow up question "Who is the Almighty leader in a charter school?"

Before an in-depth explanation, I'm certain you are wondering *What is the author's opinion about charter school leadership?* Well, I'm so glad you asked. This is my personal view: A charter school should not be controlled by just one individual. No one person should hold the keys to the charter school kingdom.

If there is only one person in charge of a charter school, this person would have to be willing to be accountable for all of the school, the students' learning, budget, staff, bylaws, parent communications, and so on. Would you want to be that guy?

Maybe that would be fine and dandy as long as it's smooth sailing. But would you want your good name—by its lonesome—in the press with a budget that went bust, or a very public complaint? Just the thought of facing an unhappy parent in the office may be enough for some of us to hyperventilate into a paper bag.

Charter schools actually have a structured design to prevent a "one-man-show." It includes a partnership of leader components. Since charter schools are all unique, there will be variances in leadership structure, too.

In *Charter Schools: The Ultimate Handbook for Parents* we will cover the basics, so consider this your scratch-and-sniff to garden-variety charter school leadership.

Governing Board

"Students cannot succeed unless the charter public school is set up to succeed—academically, financially, and organizationally."

—*National Charter School Institute*

District public schools are centrally governed by the district board of education, while charter schools are governed by an independent board of directors.

We will use the terms governing board, governing council, operating council, and operating board interchangeably to describe this entity.

The governing board is composed of elected or appointed members that write the school's charter and bylaws, and make other grand decisions. A charter school board is held accountable for everything that happens at their school, especially student achievement, fiscal and operational matters, and the execution of the mission statement. The board reports on this to its charter authorizer (*see chapter 27*).

In some cases, the school hires an outside education management organization (EMO) or charter management organization (CMO) to operate the school. Such hired services still do not forfeit the responsibility of the school board, which is still in ultimate control.

A strategic plan is created by the board to help define and prioritize goals, as well as communicate the direction of the school.

Depending on the charter, the serving board members can be parents of the school, community members, school administrators, and teachers. Some school board compositions are designed with all parent board members, others all community volunteers, and most often a mix of all of the above. Teachers and administrators are most often nonvoting members of the board, but that is more the exception than the rule.

The National Governors Association states that the best charter board includes people who are "not only are supportive of its mission and vision but who also bring a wide array of skills and knowledge, in areas such as finance, real estate, education and curriculum, and community."

The governing board is the *heart* of a charter school. Decisions made by the board affect the school's general well-being. A fit governing council can lead a school to amazing performances, while an unhealthy board is as serious as artery plaque to the charter body.

A governing board's job is to govern.

Charter school governance resources are available from National Charter Schools Institute.

Recommended reads:

THE SEVEN OUTS: STRATEGIC PLANNING MADE EASY FOR CHARTER SCHOOLS, by Brian L. Carpenter, Ph.D.

The Charter School Board University: an Introduction to Effective Charter School Governance, by Brian L. Carpenter, Ph.D.

Charter School Director

Let's do some additional name-calling of this role: school principal, head of school, dean, administrator, and chief executive officer. There are more titles, but this should suffice.

The charter school director is the executive of the school, and is hired by its operating council. The director accepts executive orders from the charter school board and is responsible for implementing them. The responsibilities of a charter school director can vary greatly depending on which school he or she is employed by. One universal duty is the charter school director's responsibility for student learning. Other assignments can include hiring and management of staff, curriculum planning, assessment results, and teacher development. A charter principal also meets with the school district or authorizer on behalf of the school.

Who leads the charter schools today?

There are rumors that charter schools are led by rookie administrators with little to no experience. Available data paints a different picture. Charter school leaders are well-seasoned professionals, but as a group, they are newer to running schools than the traditional peers. This makes sense since charter schools have been in existence for less than twenty years—much less in some states. Most state laws do not require charter school directors to be licensed public school administrators.

According to a 2008 study by the National Charter School Research Project, 80% of charter directors have degrees in education, and roughly the same percentage have taken courses in education leadership, curriculum, instruction, education law, and child development.

Leading a successful charter school requires a unique skill set than managing a district school. Due to the school's entrepreneurial nature, such a person needs to have strong business skills as much as education expertise. In addition to the curricular challenges any public school may face, charters must manage their own budgets, recruit staff, and produce high academic achievement. Many charter school directors confront these issues while working with large numbers of students whose prior school experience is sadly lacking.

In other words, although the formal background requirements may be fewer for a charter director, the professional obligations exceed what is expected of a conventional public school principal.

What do some of the successful charter schools look for when seeking to fill a school leadership position? Here are a couple of examples:

KIPP, the Knowledge Is Power Program, seeks individuals who are:

- student-focused
- relentless achievers
- people-oriented
- self-aware
- adaptable
- critical thinkers and decision makers
- strong communicators
- organized
- inspirational leaders
- instructional leaders

Achievement First looks for leaders with these values:
- commitment to mission
- focus on Excellence
- people-oriented
- instructional leadership
- constant learning
- communication
- organization and planning
- problem-solving
- character
- vision and inspiration
- management and delegation

I have yet to meet a charter school principal that is not hands-on in his or her school. There is usually an open-door policy for any student or parent. I recently met one charter director who kept his desk in the hallway to be available to the students. One can also imagine there is a different student behavior while the principal is watching.

When charter school administrators are asked in what other regard he or she spends their time, the recurring answer is—with the parents! A charter school director really must be a people person. Parent/administration communication is highly valuable in a charter school. A director will sometimes contact a parent to communicate student needs or situations. Other times he or she will contact a parent to ask for input on a topic, or recruit volunteers for a project.

The parents are often not afraid of using their voice boxes for communication either, whether the question is why little Joey is not in advanced math or why do we not have a school bus. Charter school parents, as a whole, are not known to be a shy bunch. When dealing with charter parents every new charter school principal should be equipped with the following: the patience of Job, a box of Kleenex—for all the tears and snotty noses, and a shovel—for all the…never mind.

The school principal is the *brain* of the charter body. I am not saying that nobody else has any. It's an analogy. The board is the heart; the CEO is the brain. The CEO/brain sends the orders to members of it the charter body (teachers and staff) about work that needs to be done.

If the brain is broken, it affects the learning.

Hired Management Organizations

Outsourcing is hardly a new concept in America today. It should not come as a surprise that management alternatives are used in the entrepreneurial public charter school environment. Less than 10% of public charter schools actually use an outside management company (per the National Charter School Research Project).

Charter schools that seek this type of leadership partner can opt for either full or partial management operations. The management company's services vary greatly depending on the agreement with the chartering district or independent charter schools. Such services may include fiscal management, administrative, curriculum guidance, insurance, purchasing, and so on. Management companies are designed to facilitate charter growth with consistent quality excellence.

Although there are similarities between Charter Management Organizations and Education Management Organizations, there are significant components that set them apart. To properly understand the relationship between charters and the leadership, it is important that we recognize the difference.

Charter Management Organizations (CMO)

Charter Management Organizations are nonprofit management organizations. Envision Schools and ASPIRE Public schools are well-known CMO charter schools. The Knowledge Is Power Program (KIPP) is technically not a CMO school, since the KIPP Foundation does not operate the schools. KIPP and schools like it are considered Entrepreneurial Charter Schools (more on this in part 6).

A CMO operates a network of charters serving a specific geographic location, school type, or academic mission. Unlike the (for-profit) Education Management Organizations (EMO), a Charter Management Organization can actually apply and hold the charter, hence "own" and operate a school.

CMOs' functions are local and centralized to the schools it serves, much like a school district, but with fewer administration layers. A CMO streamlines the charter operational functions according to its business model and can therefore replicate proven successes effectively. Similar to a franchise relationship, the charters purchase services from the CMO, and in return receive a consistency with built-in quality control. Since the charter management company's mission and operations are specifically for charter schools, its products and services are customized for this environment.

A CMO typically charges the charter school a set percentage of the "per pupil revenue" for its services. Oftentimes this fee does not cover the entire cost of services, and the nonprofit CMO relies on grants and philanthropic dollars to make up for the difference. All of these finance categories require a CMO to conduct research before opening a charter to set itself up for proper funding. The management company will look for community needs for additional school options, charter friendliness of the authorizer and citizens, per pupil revenue (which varies greatly in our nation), and facility availability. A management company's financial livelihood lies within its own ability on being frugal with existing funds, yet producing excellence in education business services.

For more information, please visit the following websites:
www.aspirepublicschools.org
www.envisonschools.org

Education Management Organizations (EMO)

Educational Management Organizations (EMO) are for-profit management companies. The practice of using this type of management services is almost as old as charter school law. Edison Learning, one of the recognized names in the EMO industry, originally only served charter schools while nowadays it does business with several traditional public school districts.

Each public school district or charter school holds a purse containing "per pupil revenue" (See part 6: Behind the Scenes, chapter 26, "Funding"). A school (or district) can choose to operate its management in-house, or contract an EMO with this money. An EMO may be hired to manage the school's operation in its entirety, or partial operations such as recruiting directors and staff, assessment administering and reporting, fiscal management, and so on. An EMO cannot actually file and hold a charter, which means a school business relationship is not an EMO ownership.

There has been a lot of debate about funding for charter schools that contract EMO's (for profit management companies). Supporters of EMOs profess that these management companies bring an entrepreneurial spirit and competitive edge to education business services. The attitude is that if an outsourcing company can provide much needed high quality services for less money, hence make a profit—let them.

EMO critics argue that use of such services will result in public bodies relinquishing control of schools. Opponents also express concern that outsourcing to EMOs will cause already limited resources to public schools to be charged in fees and profits for additional layers of administration.

This debate has even taken shape as to whether or not charter schools that use a for-profit management company should receive public funding for essentials, such as a school building. The greatest misconception in such debates is regarding asset ownership and *who* in the school/management relationship is for-profit and who is not.

Contrary to urban legend, contracting a for-profit education management company does not make a school for-profit. Here is why:

Example: Let's say that a nonprofit charity organization, "Feed the Kids," outsources its call center to a for-profit answering service. Such contract of services does not make "Feed the Kids" a for-profit corporation, nor does it make the answering service a shareholder of "Feed the Kids." All it means is that the answering service, although for profit, is a hired company that does business with "Feed the Kids," a nonprofit organization.

The same goes for public schools that outsource to a management company. A nonprofit public school that does business with a company that has a for-profit taxpaying profile does not change the tax-exempt status of the school, nor does it make the for-profit business a shareholder in the school's assets. Therefore, ex. a building is owned by the school, not the outsourcing company.

One likely reason why EMOs receive criticism is due to the very nature of how it does business. If a person or company can provide quality professional services on the same budget as the other public schools, but with a savings margin to make a company profit, some people in the education business become self-conscious. If you then start waving around the term "taxpayer funds" regarding that savings, you have activated a political hot button.

For more information, please visit the following Web sites:
www.edisonlearning.org
www.whitehatmanagement.com

Read more in part 6: Behind the Scenes.

CHAPTER 5

Teachers and Staff

"Mrs. Mary Campbell. She was my son's first grade teacher. It was the first year for this new charter school and many amenities were still on the wish list—like a school building.

But my boy did not complain about being taught in a trailer, nor about lacking a cafeteria, school library, or a playground. Who would pay attention to those details when you got to hang out with someone as amazing as Mrs. Campbell? He always described her as if he was comparing her with a superhero. She had glasses that made her real smart, sweatshirts that showed the seasons, and had superpowers that were previously only possessed by grandma…and maybe the 'president of the United States of Colorado.'

Come to think of it, Mrs. Mary Campbell was a super hero. When my son came to her classroom, she did not view him as the lump of coal that the naked eye would have. No, he was a diamond in the rough—and with a little of this, that and an awful lot of the other—she could make you see it too."

—"The Wind Beneath My Charter School's Wings," *2008 blog*, by Karin Piper www.yourhub.com, "How Swede It Is"

Teachers are amazing individuals to begin with. They spend at least the same amount of time educating themselves as many highly paid career professionals. Their genuine love for contributing to the common good of other people's children sets them apart from the crowd. So when we single out *charter* school teachers, it is not with disrespect to other professionals within the field, but for the sake of understanding the uniqueness of this role.

In the following pages, we will discuss the sacrifices made by teachers to work at a charter school, plus the perks. We will also address one of the most commonly asked questions, "Are charter school teachers qualified?"

Staff

On the top of the list of perks of being a charter school is the fact that the school has more freedom in whom to hire. This truly is a significant key to the success of the schools. A charter school's curricular focus and unique function are dependent on being able to hire the right staff to meet the needs of that particular environment. This is not just about teachers, but the remainder of the school employees as well.

For example, when a charter school with a technology focus is seeking a front office administrator, it may be important that this person be savvy or up-to-date on the tools required for the job. A different charter school with, let's say, a mission and curricula concentrated around foreign language integration may have different needs.

The staff at a charter school is usually bare bones compared to what we are used to seeing at the traditional levels. It comes down to cost (*see chapter 26*). I recently toured a fairly new STEM (Science, Technology, Engineering, and Math) charter school. Patiently awaiting the completion of their permanent building, the small staff is huddled so closely, they cannot stretch both arms out without smacking a colleague on the head. It did not take long before I had the explanation to both the space issue and the small office staff.

"We'd rather buy up-to-date technology equipment and give our teachers higher salaries than fill our back office with employees," says Erin Kane (founding parent of American Academy). "The permanent building is the next item on the expense priority list. To make sure we (American Academy) have funds available for future bond payments, we save money now by being in tighter quarters."

That's a pretty typical attitude of charter school leadership. Money is tight, and staff is expensive. Unless a budget line item has a direct impact on student learning, it is not on the "must have list." But if an office is run by a small staff, it needs to be a highly effective group.

There are many times I have watched the front desk guru at Parker Core Knowledge Charter School (CO) fly from phones, to copier, to students with forgotten lunchboxes, to icing playground boo-boos. In six years I have yet to see Miss Sara have a grouchy, bad day. Her kids have graduated from the school, and she could by all means have found a higher paying job elsewhere. Her dedication to the school and its kids is what makes her an MVP of her profession.

In addition to paid staff, charter schools receive much help from the enrolled families (*see chapters 22, 23, and 24*). A small school staff does not imply that there is less work. Schools have different philosophies on parental involvement in the back office. While many appreciate volunteers that man the copier, type newsletters, or answer the phones—others prefer volunteer efforts to be elsewhere in the school.

Teachers

People who enter into the teaching profession have qualities that the rest of us marvel at. I have thrown two-hour long birthday parties with the aid of hired professionals for ten kids and thought that was tough. Imagine seeing other people's ankle biters from morning to afternoon, five days a week! That takes some tenacity.

When the subject of charter school teachers and sacrifices they make come up, the same recurring question follows: are charter school teachers qualified? That's a fair question; the answer is—YES—charter school teachers are both pedigreed and competent. A better question is "What makes a (charter) school teacher qualified?"

Although state laws vary in requirements for charter school teacher certifications, many such teachers do have such credentials. And don't think that those that don't have a license were just picked off the street either. All charter educators must meet the national legal requirements (No Child Left Behind Act), which describe "Highly Qualified Teachers." What does that mean?

In general, a "highly qualified" teacher must either:

• Have obtained full State certification as a teacher or passed the State teacher licensing examination and hold a license to teach in the State, and may not have had certification or licensure requirements waived on an emergency, temporary, or provisional basis.

or

• Hold a bachelor's degree; and have demonstrated subject matter competency in each of the academic subjects in which the teacher teaches, in a manner determined by the State.

Furthermore, if charter school teachers were not qualified to teach, then why do so many charter schools turn out such highly educated students? What this means is that a charter school could, for example, hire a retired NASA engineer to teach science, or a master pianist to teach music, or a university professor in American literature to teach Language Arts—as long as their professional background makes them a "highly qualified teacher" according to the above description.

Does this mean that these folks originally went to school to become educators? No. More likely they went to school to specialize themselves within a field where they gained tremendous experience, and now they want to teach our kids.

Does this mean that they are less effective of a teacher than those who went to school for that purpose? That is a highly debatable topic. While you conclude your own opinion I want to add this: Simply because a teacher holds the right title on paper, does that mean he or she can teach every subject, even those that are not of personal strength or interest? Shall a person who has more specialized experience within a topic of his or her teaching field be less compensated than the professional who became a teacher via the traditional route? Do educators really become better when they gain additional broad-spectrum degrees under their belt? Or do teachers, like students, get better at school through gaining an interest in attaining and sharing knowledge? Is learning to teach what a textbook reads more efficient than teaching from personal experience and pursuit?

Here is an illustration:

Would you want your child taught by this dream team?

• **Reading:** Oprah Winfrey (Tennessee State University, speech and performing arts)

• **Writing:** Charles Dickens (Rome Dame School in Chatham, Clover

Lane Academy, Wellington House Academy, continued self-education by employment)

• **Math:** Albert Einstein (Luitpold Gymnasium, Eidgenössische Polytechnische Schule, Einstein was a teacher at Princeton University and a *union* member.)

• **Science:** Sir Isaac Newton (Free Grammar school, studied law at Trinity College Cambridge)

• **History:** Jesus of Nazareth (taught in the temple from the age of twelve, knew the past and the future)

• **Rhetoric and political science:** President Obama (fill this in with the U.S. president of your choice)

• **Art:** Georgia O'Keefe (Chatham Protestant Episcopal Institute in Williamsburg, Art Institute of Chicago, Art Students League in New York).

• **Music:** Herbie Hancock (famous pianist)

What do these individuals in the fictional example above have in common?

They are/were all undisputed specialists within their field, but may be more likely to possess the credentials of teaching in a charter school than in today's district schools. Even in the case of the incredible mathematician Albert Einstein, he may not have held proper licensing in your state, which would be a prerequisite for teaching K-12 education.

What is the disadvantage of teaching at a charter school?

While striking it rich is not a normal motivator to become a teacher, consider that public charter teachers generally make less than the conventional peer. A 2008 Colorado Department of Education income gap analysis shows the average income of a traditional Colorado public school teacher at $44,000, while the public charter school teacher earns an average annual salary of $33,000.

Since charter school funding is still modest, and many charters must spend part of their operating funds on facilities, budgets have to bet set with less money (*see chapter 26*). Most charter schools voice that they wish they could spend more on salaries, but are not able.

The charter teacher should not assume availability of SMART boards and ELMO technology, or other tools that are becoming common to the trade. Working in makeshift classrooms and compromising may be a part of the deal, especially if the charter is new. Many charter teachers take on additional responsibilities at the school, like directing traffic during car pool hours, working the lunchroom, or taking turns as recess aids. Sometimes they do so for extra pay, in instances like tutoring or after-school programs. Other times it is once more as a contribution to the school and its families.

So why do teacher choose charter schools? Charter schools are not just public school choice for the students, but also for the teachers.

Here are some of the common general replies:

"Charter schools are public schools. This makes it possible for a teacher to remain working in such an environment, while not being required to join a union."

"Since there are fewer regulations in regards to curricula and teaching tools, charter teachers feel empowered and given increased flexibility in how to reach the students. Teachers also serve as representatives on many governing boards and feel that they have an active voice in their schools."

Charter educators often comment on the positive aspect of parent-teacher relationships. Some charter schools even have the parent, student, and teacher sign an agreement that shows the expectations of this relationship prior to enrollment. Other schools have a minimum of family volunteer hours written into their charter bylaws and presented in the parent handbook.

One educator of an urban charter school said:

"It works like a tripod. If all three parties (parent, student, and teacher) live up to the agreement, it almost always equals student success. Should a teacher not deliver his or her end of the bargain, he or she will be out of a job. If a student does not want to be here, or is resistant to participation, we work with the parent and the teacher to improve the behavior of the child." The educator took a breath and shook his head. "The trouble is when a parent wants nothing to do with the program. That's when it's almost hopeless."

The teacher added an example of a student whose biological mother just returned into the picture. The mom feels that it is too big of a commitment for her to be involved in her child's school and wants him to attend the failing neighborhood school because it is easier. The boy has made continuous emotional pleas to his mother to keep him at his charter school. Her son is slotted to be the first in the family to graduate high school. But, if the legal guardian of a child withdraws the student, there is nothing the school can do.

Classroom sizes and discipline codes are another reason teachers opt for a chartered employer. Feeling safe in a school environment is good for everyone involved. The more intimate milieu makes it easier for the teacher to get to know each child and therefore feel connected and effective.

A significant number of charter school teachers add that they keep or have kept their own children enrolled at the school where they teach, because they believe in its mission statement and comfortable with the entire school family.

Teachers are the arms and legs of a charter school body. They are the extension of the academic body, which connects with the student, and directly delivers what he or she is learning. This is why charter schools focus so much time, effort, and as much of its resources as possible on teachers.

Why Do I Choose to Work as an Educator for a Charter School?

"In my almost fifteen years of working with youth I have only spent one year in what would be labeled as a 'traditional' public school. Even then though, I was a teacher in a 'nontraditional' subject – theatre arts. I currently serve as a 'site administrator' (known as a dean by students) for Hope Online Learning Academy Co-Op. Hope Online is a unique charter school in Colorado. I choose to work for a charter school for a couple of reasons.

My first reason is that I believe the concept of freedom of choice drives competition, and healthy competition inspires creativity and excellence. This can be applied to the pursuit of quality education. When parents can make choices about where to send their students and educators can make choices about where to focus their efforts, then our educational institutions must step up to the plate and be held accountable for the quality of education that we produce. I believe the result can and will benefit the student in the end.

My second reason for working as an educator at a charter school is the increased flexibility that it offers for 'how' we reach students. As a charter school we can use more 'nontraditional' methods to help 'nontraditional' students meet their potential and exceed their expectations. Our particular charter school chooses to focus on students that are 'at-risk and underserved' and we use online technology as the means to meet students' needs. A charter school can develop a certain personality to address the specific needs of a specific branch of a student population.

I do not believe one school can be the answer for every student in their neighborhood. We must look at educational solutions that are more comprehensive then what lies simply within a single school building. With a combination of choice, flexibility, quality, and a global approach, the educational system in our country can truly reach an equitable balance for all students.

Every child learns differently and communicates what he or she learns differently. Why shouldn't we have institutions of learning that accommodate those varieties? As soon as you try to be 'THE answer' for 'all students' then you are doomed to miss someone and that student will get 'left behind.'

As an individual educator I am not the solution, but I am one part of the solution as I work with a unique charter school.

This is why I choose to work as an educator for a charter school."

—Michael E. Udlock, site administrator for Hope Online

Interview with Laura Bender, middle school math teacher:

Nosy author: Why do you teach at Parker Core Knowledge and what drives your passion for teaching math?

LB: I wasn't a Core Knowledge supporter when I started. But I am now! I am so fortunate to be a Core Knowledge middle school teacher, because the students who come from the Core Knowledge elementary program have such an amazing foundation of knowledge. These students are well rounded, eager to learn, and used to hard work and discipline. They come to my seventh grade classroom willing to ask questions and participate in math discussions. With my small classroom size, I am able to get to know each student's strengths and weaknesses, and that helps me support them in their learning process. Parents work with me as a team and we both have their child's best interests at heart. I also teach eighth grade math, and at our school's eighth grade graduation, I look at each student and feel such a sense of accomplishment as I realize how much they've learned and grown in their two years with me. If someone wants to become a teacher because it allows him or her to touch a child's life and really make a difference, I would highly recommend becoming a charter school teacher. It is the best job in the world.

I have a passion for teaching math. I have a degree in mechanical engineering, and spent twenty years in the engineering field—as an analyst, customer support, and technical writer. When I started teaching, I thought that my primary reason for teaching math was to encourage girls to attain their best in the subject. I wanted to be a role model. But now I see how vital math understanding is to our children's ability to compete internationally, in our global society. When my daughter was in third grade in the public school system (not a charter school), she told me that her teacher didn't like math. I asked her how she knew, and she said that when her teacher taught other subjects, her voice sounded really fun. But when she taught math, her voice got very dull and boring. What a shame! It was then that I realized that people who love math (like me!) should be the ones teaching it. How can a child love math when their teacher makes it obvious that it is not interesting? I love math, and even though my students sometimes tease me about what a "nerd" I am, they admit that they'd rather be in my classroom learning math then with any other teacher.

Nosy author: Why a charter school?

LB: I have so many reasons for teaching in a charter school—first and foremost being the smaller classrooms. Because of the smaller classrooms, I am able to know the students well. I joke with parents "I know what they have for lunch!" and it's not far from the truth. I will never forget going to my son's middle school (not a charter school) for parent-teacher conferences in the fall. He had been in school for more than two months. I asked specifically about his behavior and contribution to the classroom. The teacher just looked at me and asked what he looked like. I tried to describe him but she just couldn't remember him specifically. From then on, I took a picture of him to conferences. It was the only way teachers knew whom I was discussing.

Another reason I love working at a charter school is the support and encouragement from school administrators. There is a willingness of teachers, tutors, and all school staff to support and encourage each and every student. Differentiation is a buzzword at all of the traditional public schools. It's just a fancy word for what we've been doing since the school opened. We work hard to meet the needs of the students. Of course we differentiate, because we know these kids so well, and they're all so different!

Nosy author: What single classroom experience has had that "this is why I teach here" kind of impact on you?

LB: I had a meeting with a parent this morning. I have taught all three of her children. We were discussing her youngest, an eighth grader, who will be leaving for high school in just a couple of months. Together with her son we discussed how he can end the year as a strong and confident student. Together we praised him, and together we admonished him to do his best. I guarantee that the student left our meeting feeling good about himself and confident in his abilities. Not everything we said was positive; he has some areas that he needs to work on, but knowing that we care meant a lot to him.

I taught a lovely young girl a few years ago. She graduated from eighth grade and then the family moved out of state. The father of the family went out of his way to contact our school and let us know that his daughter had decided to study engineering in college. I taught his daughter Algebra I, and she wasn't my strongest student, but she was one of the most dedicated students I have taught. She worked and worked until she understood each concept. I know that she left our school confident and strong, and I can't help but think that I may have helped influence her to decide on a math-based career.

—Laurie Bender is middle school math teacher at Parker Core Knowledge Charter School (CO). She is a degreed mechanical engineer who possesses two decades of professional engineering experience. She is an example of many professionals who opt to teach in specialized subjects with a passion for teaching.

Teacher's Desk: What Val Taught Me

"I miss Val. Val was an ornery girl when I first met her. I mistook her for a he because of her gender-bending style. But she kept me on my toes, and she grew into a wonderful student by the time she graduated last year. Her attendance was nearly perfect, her skill levels rose, and I had to move her out of remedial classes. She consistently made honor roll, reached her required benchmarks and credits to graduate, and became a school leader.

Most important, Val taught me it was all right to tell my students I love them. At the end of the day I taught a math class that she attended. Students tend to be highly distractible the last period of the day and mathematics takes a lot of focus. My class was well behaved one day as I modeled problem solving. Val passed me a note that said, 'I love you, but this is so boring.' She spelled every word correctly, too! After that day, I used her spontaneous 'I love you' to my students. With my classroom management style of 'no nonsense,' this was a perfect companion.

After working at a large, impersonal Denver high school, being at our little school and hearing 'I love you' float through the halls instead of profanities during passing periods was true joy. When many of my at-risk students hear 'I love you' from a friend or teacher, that may very well be the only 'I love you' they hear for a month or more. Val spread joy into many of our lives and truly added value to our school culture.

It was easy to add something to our school culture as the rules were already in place on the use of profanity in our building. If a student uses profanity, a profanity 'report' is issued for the student to hand copy and present to the offended staff. If the report, which discusses the history of public utterances of profanity, is not returned to the offended staff, the student will not earn credit nor receive a passing grade for that six-week period."

—*Kathleen Kullback is a licensed special educator teaching remedial classes at Colorado High School Charter, an alternative school. She holds a MA in administration and policy from the University of Colorado at Denver and is a former candidate for the Colorado State Board of Education.*

To view the profanity report and this blog in full, visit http://backboneamerica.net/2009/01/30/teachers-desk-what-val-taught-me/.

"When I entered kindergarten in the early 1980s, my parents didn't send me to our neighborhood school. They said it lacked 'values education,' had large classes, and did not stress academics. Instead, they scrimped to send me to parochial school until we could move to a city with better schools. It was the 'haves' and 'have-nots': parents who couldn't afford private school or a home elsewhere *had no choice.*

Fast forward to 2009: Parents have choices and options when it comes to their child's education. Students at Trillium Academy come from over twenty-five different school districts, and their parents choose Trillium for myriad reasons.

Our fine arts curriculum includes visual art, drama, music, Spanish, physical education, and technology for all students. We believe in educating the whole child, and our charter contract ensures the fine arts will *not* be cut. It is the exact opposite in many local districts. I can't tell you how many high school students come to Trillium without any prior experience to any form of art.

We also use a Montessori philosophy of differentiated instruction to allow students to achieve at their own pace. Because classes are small, we're able to closely monitor individual achievement. Regardless of their prior academic record, we place high expectations on *all* students.

In our classrooms, it's common to see a general education teacher working with one cluster of children, a special education teacher with a small group, and a team of students working independently. Yes, assessments show our approach *is* successful.

Charter schools must live up to stringent state regulations, legislative expectations, and state school board scrutiny. Charters must also answer to their educational service providers, their school board, and the entity—usually a state university or community college—that grants their charter contract.

Before charters, underperforming districts received funding, regardless. Today, funding follows the pupil. Successful schools attract students, and failing schools face consequences for the first time in our history. If a charter school does not perform, it is closed.

Open seven years now, Trillium has waiting lists in many grades, and parents weep with joy when their names are called to fill open seats. Many charters face this situation, and families often register at multiple schools, desperate to get into at least one.

I'm proud to be making a difference in the lives of children. I'm proud to teach at a charter school."

—*Lisa Koski, teacher, grades 2-3, Trillium Academy (MI), 2005 Michigan Charter Teacher of the Year*

CHAPTER 6

The Students

This is the main event. It's what it's all about—the kids! Without student enrollment, there is no purpose for any school.

But who is a charter school student? There are two distinctly contradicting rumors; one that charter kids are all juvenile delinquents from inner city, gang-ridden neighborhoods, the other that charter schools only enroll the brightest, wealthiest, and most affluent kids of the posh suburbs. So which one is it?

Well, which demographic group is in your neighborhood schools? That is who is in your local charter schools. Since charter schools are public schools and follow antidiscrimination laws, the diversity of charter schools is similar to the ones in the nearby area. If a community is largely Hispanic, black, white, or purple, that's what can be expected in your area charter schools. Sure, there are some families that go out of their way to out-of-district schools to enroll their kids in a school they believe in. But that's hardly unique to charter schools, and it's usually a sign that a school offers certain academic desirables, nothing else.

There are charters specifically designed for the gifted and talented, or to help inner city kids that are entangled in the justice system. But a few charter schools cannot be used to profile an entire nation of students, nor the whole spectrum of charter school purpose. Since charter schools cannot (by law) discriminate by race—ethnicity, gender, income, and so on—it assures that public school choice is available for everyone.

When a charter is created it is done so to meet needs relevant to the kids in that particular community. It is not the kids who are handpicked to meet the need of the school. Keep the phrase "choice" in mind when you think about charter school students. There is a reason they attend that particular school. Some parents enroll their children in the neighborhood school by default because they are unaware of alternatives. In a charter school, the parent had to go out of their way to register and enroll the child. It is a truly conscious decision.

So why would a parent place a child in a chartered public school versus the traditional? Usually the parent is seeking something different for the child. Perhaps the student has needs that are not easily met in the broader purpose environment of a conventional school. Other times it is a curriculum, classroom size, or higher quality reputation that adds to the appeal. In low performing public school areas parents may enroll a child into a charter school due to higher graduation rates, to give the student the opportunity to go to college, or better prepare for a vocation. In areas where the neighborhood schools already have good performance, a parent's motivation may be geared toward allowing him or her to learn at a different pace, or study a certain program that is not offered in a general environment (*see parent testimonials, part 1*).

What makes a charter school desirable for a student or parent is not limited to the information above. These examples do, however, show that although charter students tend to be the kids whose needs fall outside the peripheral boundaries of mass-produced learning, one cannot accurately stereotype charter student demographics any more than traditional schools.

Here are a few statements from charter school kids around the nation on the topic of what a charter school provides for them:

"I had many choices of choosing a school that would fit my needs. My mom wanted a school that my teachers would help me and my teammates. Since I did not know any school, I asked my former principal, Mr. Harrison, if he could help me find a school. Since Mrs. Kullback, my former teacher, taught at both my previous middle school and a high school, she recommended her high school, Colorado High School Charter. One day I had a chance to visit and my experience was great. That's why I made the decision to go to Colorado High School Charter. The reason why I am here is because I know that I can be someone with a good education. I'm here because I have the support that I need for my future.

During my visit through this school I thought this would be the high school to graduate from. I like this school because the teachers help me a lot. The teachers and staff make me feel welcome once I entered school. When you ask a question, the teachers will help you or if you have a problem, they will help you solve it. I like how the system works here.

Colorado High School Charter helped me realize that I could graduate from school and become someone with a great desire to succeed. Basically, I like to attend school every day but sometimes I have to miss school, even though I don't like to, but my eyesight causes me to miss because of my vision. I like how teachers and staff help and because they know that I have an IEP (Individual Education Plan), they help me to pass each class. I like it that they understand my vision problem. Since I read slowly, they give me more time to finish my schoolwork.

Colorado High School Charter is a school that I would recommend to my friends or someone else because they (the teachers) do help you succeed and help you in school a lot. This is why I decided to attend Colorado High School Charter. My mom is so proud of me that I will graduate this year. My dream is to graduate from Colorado High School Charter and I will do it with the help of teachers and staff."

—Maria Rodriguez, Colorado Charter High School (CO) Age 18

"I attended IDEA College Preparatory Donna for seven years and I am currently a freshman at Tufts University in Medford, Massachusetts. I hope to pursue a double major in chemical engineering and history or political science.

I first heard of IDEA from my fifth grade teacher, Seth Cohen, when I was attending elementary school in Donna, Texas. I had no intention of attending IDEA, but after so much insisting on my mother's behalf, I decided to give it a shot.

Since then, IDEA has done everything within its power to help me get to where I am at today, in college. I am the first in my family to attend college. Both my family and IDEA have been very supportive throughout this journey of mine.

IDEA did everything it could have possibly done to prepare me for college.

As I am finishing up my first year, I feel that college was everything I was expecting and everything my high school teachers said it would be.

I feel that the rigors of college are a lot easier to handle, thanks to all of the exceptionally hard work that IDEA had assigned me throughout my high school years. Adjusting to college life has been fairly easy for me, except for a couple things here and there, such as learning to use the subway system here at Tufts, the food, the climate change (Massachusetts is cold!), and the fact that I miss my family and friends.

Since I've been here at Tufts University, I have had the opportunity to experience Boston, learn about different people, and share my stories with others.

I can say without a doubt that if I had not attended IDEA I would not be here at Tufts University. Upon graduating from Tufts, I plan to give back to the community that has given me so much. I want to continue my education by attending the Harvard Law School and hopefully someday serve as representative for the area that I come from or serve as justice on the United States Supreme Court.

Thanks to IDEA Public Schools many underprivileged students have an equal opportunity to learn, receive a high quality education, and pursue their dreams and ambitions."

—*Zanyace Q. Aguiñaga, Class of 2008 IDEA College Preparatory Donna*

"I would like to spend a moment to address the Ridgeview experience, as I have been at this school for nearly four years. I have had the opportunity to watch the school expand and change principals, to enjoy learning about all sorts of different things, from the Japanese Charter Oath, to the creation of recombinant DNA, to the proof of the Pythagorean Theorem, but most of all, to be part of the Ridgeview community.

When I first came to Ridgeview, I was in sixth grade, coming out of another school that I had been in for four weeks. I expected an apathetic teacher, an apathetic student body, and a boring book to read with apathetic characters (which I would, by the way, be apathetic to). I was completely wrong. My teacher at the time was Mrs. Nazeck (although then, she was Miss Kretschmer). Not only was she extremely intelligent, not only was she ever helpful, she was the protector and corrector of every student. On those rare occasions when there was a kid who was mean to another (no matter who it was), she would scold and pink slip him. I speak of her, because she was my first teacher at RCS, but I find that every teacher since has behaved the same. The teachers protect the weak and correct the bullies, so that every student has the ability to grow in character and intellect.

Very soon after I came to Ridgeview, I realized that, for the first time since I moved to Colorado, I was not alone among my peers. Whenever there were bullies at Ridgeview (although they were few and far between), it was not only the teachers who stepped in and stopped them, but the virtuous students did so as well. I remember those times when sweet little Jasmine would step in whenever a student would get offended or be upset.

I used to find that I was incompatible with most kids due to my dissimilarity from them. When I came to Ridgeview, I found that the only similarity I needed to have was a willingness to be a good person and a good friend. Here at Ridgeview, I found a warm and welcoming home among the students.

Four years that I might have spent in apathy and depression, I spent with my correctors, protectors, encouragers, and stabilizers. Four years that I might have spent watching the clock, waiting to graduate, I spent learning and growing. I believe credit should be given where credit is due. I would very much like to thank the Ridgeview community now for giving me these four years. The education I have thus far received will be with me forever."

—*Ariel Hoffman, Ridgeview Classical (CO)*

"When I grow up, I want to be an environmentalist to help save animals in danger.

My school, *The Classical Academy*, is helping me fulfill my dream with the subjects that are being taught. Some of the main character traits we talk about here at TCA are compassion, responsibility, and diligence.

To begin, our school is built on having compassion for others. Being a student in this school has helped me to understand about helping others. I have a deep sense of compassion for animals. For years people have been polluting our oceans. They just throw trash into the ocean to get rid of it. When plastic rings are thrown into the ocean from six packs of cans, they can sometimes get stuck on dolphin's beaks and starve them if they can't get it off in time to eat.

Responsibility is another great character trait that we learn here at TCA. Our elementary school has a 'Green Team.' They meet every week to talk about environmental issues, including pollution. They have set up recycling bins to recycle instead of throwing the trash into a can to be buried underground. We all need to take responsibility for our garbage.

Finally, when preparing to be an environmentalist, a person needs to have perseverance to keep up their studies. The Classical Academy teaches us many valuable subjects. We are learning science, history, math, and computer. A student needs to work hard to do well in all of the different subjects.

In conclusion, I have learned some great character traits at my charter school that will help me become a better adult. In addition to the character traits that I have mentioned, I have learned about several others. I have also learned great ways to help our animals, and I have developed a passion for learning. All of these wonderful ideas are what make The Classical Academy the best education that I could have to become the best person that I can be, and the best environmentalist I can be."

—*Kayla Summers, The Classical Academy (CO), "The Dream Yet to Come"*

"Tony's Turn Around"

Tony, a second grader attending Hope Online at Roca Fuerte Learning Center, colors with measured precision and focus. He leans into his picture and seems to tune out the activity swirling around him in Ms. Morgan's class. Perhaps it is because Tony is on a mission—to complete the second grade and move on to third grade, with an eye on seventh grade as soon as possible.

"Obviously, we would not encourage Tony to advance beyond a level that would be good for him, academically or socially," insists his mentor, Virginia Morgan. "But, Tony has made a complete turnaround in his attitude since he realized how he can progress through the Hope Online program, and we are determined to help him achieve."

Just a few months ago, it looked as though Tony was not going to succeed at Roca Fuerte or anywhere else because of his agitating and disruptive behavior in class. Despite his gentle smile, Tony bullied other children, regardless of their age. He caused so much concern that he was moved to another classroom with hopes that he would fit in better. But, according to Ms. Morgan, he continued picking fights with classmates and discussing inappropriate topics such as guns and drugs.

"It was a very frustrating time," recalls Ms. Morgan. "I worked with our Hope Online teacher and just kept plugging away with him, especially as I realized some of the crises that fostered his behavior. He desperately wanted to feel equal to the other kids." Then came the day that Tony took notice of the lessons his older classmates were completing. He asked his teacher if he could do the same work. She explained that he could not skip lessons but that he could work at his own pace to advance. Finally, Tony's attention and ambition were captured.

Since that day, Tony has studied relentlessly. With the help of his mentor and the statistics that track his performance and progress, Tony understands the steps toward earning the privilege of higher-level work. He asks for permission to use his breaks to study, and he is committed to redoing any lessons that were not up to standard. Tony is clearly motivated to pass his lessons and move ahead. Starting fights no longer interests him."

—HOPE Online (CO)

CHAPTER 7

The Parents

"**What is the difference between a charter school mom and a pit bull?**

One is legal to unleash in Douglas County.

Whoever answered lipstick would be wrong. If you have ever been in a charter school car pool line, you'd notice that we are more likely to wear pajamas in public and our kid's breakfast wiped on our sleeves than lipstick.

We do have a couple of similar traits with pit bulls though. The most infamous of such is probably the habit of fiercely fighting for our little ones and their environment."

— "Charter School Moms and Pit Bulls," *blog by Karin Piper 2008*

Ah yes, charter school moms—and dads—have a reputation that precedes them.

They are known for their loyalty, generosity, dedication and intensity they bring to their children's school. Charter school parents are few but mighty and represent the huge impact a small body of dedicated folks can have on education. From starting schools to volunteering in the lunchroom, there is no job too big or too small for these folks. Charter school parents are a force to be reckoned with.

Just like charter kids, their parents come in all kinds. There are some parents who have little to do with their school of choice, where as others are "two-feet-in" kinds of people. I suspect that if you are a prospective charter school parent reading this book, you may be the latter. So let's have a little fun with charter school parent stereotyping (some true, others we'll deny). View the following pages as a self-discovery guide for readers who suspect they may be potential give-it-all-you've-got kind of charter school parents.

You might be a charter school parent if …

…you are a bona fide "label-reader."

When going down the aisle of the grocery store you are presented with a vast ocean of options. It seems like there is a flavor, brand, and price to suit most everyone's taste. While marketing and cost may play some part, there are plenty of parents who look beyond the façade and turn the packaging around for a closer look at the fine print.

Congratulations if this fits your description: you just might be a charter school parent. A stereotypical charter school parent is no stranger to making conscious decisions. Pediatricians and dentists are usually not chosen by accident; neither is junior's education.

Enrolling a child in a school without checking its content is like buying clothes without specifying a size. How do you know it fits?

Since a letter of intent needs to be completed prior to enrolling a student in a charter school, all kids attending such a school are there very much by parental choice. While a traditional neighborhood school is commonly the first consideration for a child of school age, parents who opt differently tend to research available education offerings (many noncharter families practice this too, of course). Some areas have multiple charter schools, which even add an element of choice among public school choice.

…you think cannot is a dirty word.

There are days I wonder if Fred W. Smith is a charter school parent. If not, he should try it. He'd fit right in. According to FedEx lore, Fred W. Smith was an undergrad student at Yale University when he penned a term paper on overnight delivery. The thought at the time was considered both naïve and absurd, since the United States Postal Service had been in business for more than two centuries and had determined the feat impossible. Fred W. Smith reckons he got a C on the later-famed paper. But people like Fred W. Smith have this filter, which sifts out the words *no*, *impossible*, *unthinkable*, and *cannot*. He's a yes, how, outside-the-USPS-box, and sure-we-can man.

When Mr. Smith received some inheritance money, he used it to materialized his C graded term paper into a multi-billion dollar delivery system. Call it gullibility, stubbornness, or stupidity—history will remember it as how the mail service world changed forever.

Suddenly it wasn't just FedEx that could deliver packages overnight. Even the United States Postal Service gained a couple of words in its vocabulary, like *priority, express, overnight*—and *maybe we can do it, after all!*

Charter school parents, like Fred W., are a bunch whose laser focus is not easily swayed. The motivating source for these parents never-say-die spirit is their kids. Charter schools are driven by parents, oftentimes even created by them. It is a world of thinking outside the box to fill unique needs in education, many which have never been addressed by the traditional environment. The word *no* has been heard so often, its effect has pretty much been worn out. The search for education solutions is like a maze, and the word *no* just means you need to find a different route. Sometimes finding that route will pave the road for scores of other schools still stuck in deadends of the maze.

The phrase *charter school parent* should probably be changed in the dictionary from a noun to a verb. Because a charter school parent is more about *doing* than just *being*.

...you secretly dream of being a school bus driver.

As the blog entry to this chapter described, car pool lines are not uncommon in charter schools. Since few charter schools have bus transportation (*see chapter 17*) getting the kids to and from school becomes the responsibility of the parents. It's rather amusing to watch the school car pool in progression. The veteran parents who have tracked a few thousand drop-offs and pick-ups usually arrange joint car pools with another family or three.

Sure, it can get a little crazy when you drive around half a dozen ankle biters every morning and afternoon, but you do it for the perks. How many other driving gigs do you know of where it is perfectly normal for the driver to wear pajama pants and curlers? And you'll be carting around some of the cutest and smartest kids in town (some of them are yours, after all). Not bad company. You will also make friends with some of those moms who are super organized and e-mail you car pool schedules complete with high def PowerPoints, phone trees, worst-case-scenario escape clauses. Trust me—these are parents well worth knowing based on their skills of coordinating a car pool alone.

These ride sharing arrangements are one well-greased transportation machine, which could serve as a car commercial anytime. If you ever wanted to know how many kids could safely fit in a _____ (car brand of choice), just watch how many kids climb out of one in the morning car line. Count the heads of kids jumping out and you will know how many seat belt options come with that make and brand. The more kids you can offer a ride to, the more families will offer a ride in return for your kids. I'm still waiting for my carpool dream vehicle to become street legal—the clown car.

...your favorite clothing retailer ends with the word uniforms.

Have you watched a stroller of twins dressed identically pull by and a swarm of strangers stop to comment on how adorable they look? It seems the more kids in the cart in the same color creepers, the more complimentary the reaction.

A similar reaction is expressed by many parents when they see an ocean of diverse public school children, dressed in a school uniform. Not all charters have uniform wear, or strict dress codes, but it is definitely not uncommon. Aside from the cute-twins effect, there are some clear advantages to united school wear from a parent's perspective. Here are a few:

Mornings are much smoother when clothing choices are limited. The "I-don't-know-what-to-wear" comments are not as frequent when you can pick the navy pants, or the navy pants.

Peer pressure to purchase expensive brand name items is virtually nonexistent. Try buying the latest fad shoes in solid white or brown with no logo. Nope, those types of dress code rules assure that every family shows up in some offbeat, no-name brand that remains anonymous.

Hand-me-downs do not go out of style. There are six years between the ages of my oldest and my youngest child. Six years make a huge difference in what's cool to wear in nonuniform schools, but in uniform schools the clothes are just as stylish as they were from day one.

Cost savings. Many families celebrate moneys saved when their kids are in uniform. Perhaps it is because impulse shopping is not as rampant if you do not have mandated school wear. Few are the times when I have heard an ecstatic mother holler down the kid's aisle that she just found the most adorable plain white polo she must buy right now!

Sure you may be a parent who is not fond of uniforms. It really does not mean that charters should be checked off the list. But if you are someone whose personal wardrobe yields rows and rows of the same shirt in a different color, you may want to consider this chapter as a possible self-diagnosis.

...you know your child's teacher's home phone number by heart.

You think that I am kidding, don't you? I am not. I recently visited a KIPP middle school where the teachers sign a contract promising to be available to students and parents day and night. These teachers hand out cell numbers and are pretty much on call 24/7. The school founder told me that there really has not been any reported abuse of this system. Suppose texting your teacher at 2 a.m. hasn't caught on as a fad yet.

A charter school really is like a family. If a parent or student is running into a snag, calling or e-mailing the teacher is not just encouraged—it's expected. If you are coming from a traditional school climate, this may take some getting used to.

Recently a teacher told me that coming from a school where she rarely saw any parents, she was stunned when she walked into a charter school classroom lined with welcoming faces. "This," she says while pointing at our kids sharing a popcorn tub in the movie theater, "never happened at my other school."

As a parent you are your charter school teacher's partner and viewed as the home component in your child's education success. Without proper communication, how can either of you be effective?

On the other side of the white board there are ways we, as charter parents, can make sure that communication is not misused. Working side by side with your child's teacher comes with a certain level of responsibility. First of all, we need to make sure we remain respectful, even when we don't agree. When we are talking about our kids, fangs and claws can accidentally come out from a well-meaning mom or dad. Addressing a concern with a teacher is a good place to start, but if you think you may be very sensitive about a subject or worried that a conversation may not be productive—please involve the director. Communication is teamwork and takes practice. Nobody is expecting perfection. But knowing your teacher's phone number, cell number, e-mail and shoe size is an awful lot of parental power. So if you become a charter school parent, be sure you use your newfound powers nicely.

...you spell volunteerism with a capital V.

If you are hankering for a really good community project, I am not sure if it is the charter school that needs you, or if you need to look for a charter. It is truly a match made in heaven. Most charter schools have a minimum volunteer hour requirement for its attending families. This doesn't mean that you need to be there unless you want to, of course. There are plenty of parents who volunteer by correcting papers at home, sending goodies for school events, precutting templates for classwork and so on. But if you are longing to belong to an organization that depends on your involvement—or wish to find like-minded thinkers—a charter school is a great place to be.

Many friends have been made between adults who contribute their time at the kid's school. Volunteerism is so rampant among charter schools that many such institutions have added "Volunteer Appreciation Day" to the schedule, which was already honoring "President's Day," "Mother's Day," and "Teacher Appreciation Week."

In conclusion

If you are a limitless, pajama clad, do-it-your-selfer with an oversized vehicle that makes decisions by pro-and-con-lists, and keep teacher phone numbers on speed dial—you just might be a charter school parent. Admission is always step one. Step two is to speed-read this book to the chapter on how to find a support group...I mean, charter school. There is no cure for desiring a charter school culture, but there is a school culture of your desire.

By finding the right charter school for your family, you will join others who are already openly expressing their comfort with public school choice. There are those that believe charter school behavior is innate. Others believe it is learned. Regardless of which philosophy you err on, there is absolutely no shame in admitting a hankering for charter schools.

In the anatomy of charter schools, *the parents are the soul.* The parts of the charter school body find a deeper meaning and efficiency with the help of the parents.

Read about what may be expected from charter school parents in chapters 12, 17, 22, and 23.

CHAPTER 8

The Community

Forty U.S. states (plus the District of Columbia) already have existing charter school law. The public perception of these schools varies greatly based on how long charter laws have been in effect, how many and how successful the schools are, and how good the communication between charter schools and its community is.

Although charter schools have been around nationally since 1991, countless individuals remain generally uninformed about this public school venture. What is even more unfortunate is that the sorts of information that seem to be spreading the fastest are misconceptions and rumors. That is not to say that it is all negative information—it is simply backwards information. For example, the most often asked question about charter schools is "Is it a private or public school?" And you'll almost certainly run across someone who will ask you why your kids can't go to the neighborhood schools like "everybody else." It is not out of ill will, it's usually because there is limited information being circulated about chartered education.

The Colorado League of Charter Schools recently conducted a survey through an independent research company, polling the general public about knowledge on charter schools. The results were interesting. Of the adults polled, 53% believed that Colorado parents should have a right to choose the public school they believe to best fit the needs of their kids. Only 16% felt confident that they "knew quite a bit" about charter schools, although 67% felt they were supportive of them. Then they were read this statement:

> "Charter schools are independent public schools that have the flexibility to be more innovative and are held accountable for improved student achievement."

After the research company asked the persons polled if charter schools were public schools, 66% of the surveyed adults answered yes. So, if only 66% of our population is aware that charter schools are public schools after they have been told so at least once, what more can we do to educate our communities about these schools?

A charter school is wise in organizing regular open house events and writing to the editors of local papers of school happenings. The more our neighbors know about what is going on inside our school buildings, the fewer the misconceptions.

In areas where charter support is thriving local businesses often sponsor school events, or support by other means. Some companies will offer internships for students of charter schools with whom they partner. It is also a common occurrence for local restaurants or school supply retailers to team with charter schools for fund raisers.

On the other side of the fence, charter school students are often required by their school to participate in a certain amount of community service hours. Not unlike the scout program, charter kids across the country pitch in to help their neighborhoods in various service projects.

In charter-supporting communities citizens tend to stay abreast and involved in current events that affect school choice. This can be especially helpful come election time if charter school related items are on the ballot. If someone does not understand the significance of a ballot issue, they are much more likely to say no. Talk to your family and friends about charter schools. The more they know, the more likely they are to be supportive.

Here is an example of a charter school which has been recognized for community involvement:

"Today's students are faced with an abundance of challenges as they enter the work place. A turbulent economy, ever-evolving technology—the ability to adapt is paramount to their success. Vigorous new schools with inventive educational programs are required in order to prepare our students. The Denver Venture School has the vision and community support to accomplish this task.

As a public charter school, the Denver Venture School prides itself on offering a real life, project based, business-oriented curriculum in a small public school environment. A diverse group of students enrolled through a lottery system, each being held to a standard of achievement. Faculty and administration refer to their students as 'scholars,' helping shape the way the students view themselves.

Juniors will ultimately spend a large portion of their school day operating a business they will plan and launch themselves, with coaching by business leaders. The resulting symbiotic relationship formed between the business community and scholars will pave the way for internships, friendships and lifelong mentors.

There is a reciprocal gain from having these future business leaders learning in the heart of our city. The Downtown Denver Area Plan, adopted by City Council in 2007, specifically cites the need for a magnet school in the core of Downtown, early childhood education opportunities, and other elements that would attract families to live in Downtown. The location of Denver Venture School is in the Curtis Park neighborhood will infuse new energy into the area, anchoring the community around a high performing public school.

When the doors of Denver Venture School opened to its first 60 scholars in August of 2008, an incredible opportunity was given to our business community. Through these young adults, we can help shape and grow—at the root level—those attributes that we seek in our own workforce. This kind of organic educational opportunity could hold the key to ensuring the vitality of our own urban core."

—*Downtown Denver Partnership Award 2008 presented to Denver Venture School (CO)*

Part 3

Expectations

In Part 3:

9. The Workload
   Will my child be challenged or have trouble keeping up?
10. Curricula
    What is the curriculum for charter schools?
11. Homework
    Whose homework is it anyway? What is expected on the home front?
12. ESL, GT, and SPED
    Do charter schools accept special-needs students?
13. Discipline
    Laying down the law
14. Dress Code
    Uniforms and dress codes
15. School Facility
    What do you mean we're in trailers? And other potential building surprises
16. Transportation
    James, home please! Your carpool arrangements
17. Character Education
    What is character education and why is it in the classroom?

OVERVIEW

- What to expect when you are expecting a charter school? As one can imagine, the standard reply is that it varies.

- Part 3 will answer some of the questions about charter school functions, which are often asked by incoming families. This is the chapter where we will discuss expected workload, what to wear, the difference between amenities and necessities, as well as learning services.

CHAPTER 9

The Workload

Since charters are designed to answer to its authorizer on two points, fiscal responsibility and academic performance, one can expect these two areas to be a keen focus of such schools.

In areas where schools have low graduation rates and performance gaps, charters tend to accelerate student learning by extended days and school years to catch up. Other charter schools, which offer choice within areas that offer existing reputable public schools, may provide honors programs and accelerated courses. Some charters may be designed to specifically aid children with special learning needs, or handicaps.

Be aware that every charter is designed with a unique twist, so learning ahead of time what will be expected of your family is a prudent step in the process. To demonstrate how different charter schools are, please refer to the sample documents below. These two different charters serve polar-opposite student demographics. One example is from KIPP, which serves largely urban areas. The other document is from The Classical Academy in Colorado Springs, CO, which is located in a suburb.

Knowledge Is Power (KIPP) Commitment to Excellence:

Teacher Commitment:
We fully commit to KIPP in the following ways:
We will arrive at KIPP every day by 7:15 a.m. (Mon.-Fri.).
We will remain at KIPP until 5:00 p.m. (Mon.-Thurs.) and 4:00 p.m. on Fridays.
We will come to KIPP on appropriate Saturdays at 9:15 a.m. and remain until 1:05 p.m.
We will teach KIPP during the summer.
We will always teach in the best way we know how and we will do whatever it takes for our students to learn.
We will always make ourselves available to students, parents, and any concern they might have.

Expectations: The Workload

We will always protect the safety, interests, and rights of all individuals in the classroom.

Failure to adhere to these commitments can lead to our removal from KIPP.
x_____

Parent's/Guardian's Commitment:
We fully commit to KIPP in the following ways:
We will make sure our child arrives at KIPP every day by 7:25 a.m. (Mon.-Fri.).
We will make arrangements so our child can remain at KIPP until 5 p.m. (Mon.-Thurs.) and 4:00 p.m. Fridays.
We will make arrangements for our child to come to KIPP on appropriate Saturdays at 9:15 a.m. and remain until 1:05 p.m.
We will ensure that our child attends KIPP summer school (June 2010).
We will always help our child in the best way we know and we will do what is right for him/her to learn. This also means that we will check our child's homework every night, let him call the teacher if there is a problem with the homework, and try to read with him/her every night.
We will always make ourselves available to our children, the school, and any concern they might have. This also means that if our child is going to miss school, we will notify the teacher as soon as possible and we will read carefully all the papers that the school sends home to us.
We will allow our child to go on earned KIPP field trips.
We will make sure our child follows the KIPP dress code.
We will understand that our child must follow the KIPP rules so as to protect the safety, interests, and rights of all individuals in the class room. We, not the school, are responsible for the behavior and actions of our child.

Failure to adhere to these commitments can cause my child to lose various KIPP privileges, spend time on "Base Camp," and can lead to my child returning to his/her home school.

x_____

Student's Commitment:
I fully commit to KIPP in the following ways:
I will arrive at KIPP every day by 7:25 a.m. (Mon.-Fri.).
I will remain at KSPA until 5 p.m. (Mon-Thu) and 4:00 p.m. Fridays
I will come to KIPP on appropriate Saturdays at 9:15 a.m. and remain until 1:05 p.m.
I will attend KIPP during summer school.
I will always work, think, and behave in the best way I know how and will do whatever it takes for me and my fellow students to learn. This also means that I will complete all my homework every night, I will call my teachers if I have a problem with the homework or a problem with coming to school, and I will raise my hand and ask questions in class if I do not understand something.
I will always make myself available to parents and teachers, and address any concerns they might have. If I make a mistake, this means I will tell the truth to my teachers and accept responsibility for my actions.
I will always behave so as to protect the safety, interests, and rights of all individuals in the classroom. This also means that I will always listen to all my KIPP teammates and give everyone my respect.
I will follow the KIPP dress code.
I am responsible for my own behavior, and I will follow the teachers' directions.

Failure to adhere to these commitments can cause me to lose various KIPP privileges, spend time on "Base Camp," and can lead to returning to my home school.

x_____

For more information about KIPP charter schools, visit www.kipp.org.

TCA Parental Letter of Understanding

"The Classical Academy exists to assist parents in their mission to develop exemplary citizens equipped with analytical thinking skills, virtuous character, and a passion for learning, all built upon a solid foundation of knowledge."

As a charter school, The Classical Academy (TCA) is a public school you choose based on a personal alignment with our mission, philosophy, and core values rather than geography. It was founded to serve a niche within the Colorado Springs community who held a different view of the proper relationship between a public school and the parents it serves. There are both benefits and sacrifices for families that choose to depart from the typical model of 100% government-funded and government-run education. This document is an attempt to highlight some of those points in order to assist you with making an informed decision about joining the TCA community. We want to be very direct and candid with you on one unwavering reality—**the TCA model will only continue to succeed if everyone who shares in the benefits is also willing to share in the sacrifices.** Please make your decision based on a realistic picture of what TCA has to offer, and whether this educational model is right for your family. We are proud of our school and the option that it presents to you. If you are in agreement with our mission, attracted to our philosophy, and welcome the high level of parental commitment and involvement that is a hallmark of our school, then we sincerely hope you will join us in this venture of educating our children.

A core distinction of TCA is the role of the parents and their relationship to the school. TCA will succeed **only** with a parent body, which has chosen NOT to abdicate their responsibility and authority to the school. Likewise, success also depends on school personnel understanding that their role is not to usurp authority that should belong to the parents. In order for this model to work, parents are asked to support the TCA mission statement, philosophy, and core values with their time, talent, and treasures. TCA has made philosophical decisions that positively impact the learning environment for our students, such as small class sizes. However, this comes at a financial cost that is further impacted by the lack of school facility funding inherent in charter schools creating a shortfall of approximately 20%. For the continued success and stability of the school, parents must understand the importance of supporting the school financially. Note that private schools of similar quality often have tuitions ranging from $5000–$15,000 per student. It is also important to understand that TCA has a distinctively defined philosophy of Classical Education that is based on a blend of Charlotte Mason ideologies, the trivium, and the Socratic Method which makes small class size imperative.

Your commitment to TCA:

As a member of the TCA parent community, I commit to the following shared values and standards:

- I will read and support the TCA Mission Statement and core values;

- I will seek opportunities to assist the teachers and coaches that are working directly with my student(s);

- I will actively participate in TCA community events and projects;

- I will support the TCA staff with a cooperative spirit and always engage them in a positive manner;

- I will support the TCA uniform policy by only purchasing clothing items consistent with those listed in the student handbook and requiring my student to dress in the appropriate attire during school hours;

- I will address any problems or issues concerning my student in accordance with the TCA conflict resolution policy;

- I will strive for a Classical Home environment in our home by maximizing reading and hands-on learning.

TCA Parental Letter of Understanding

I acknowledge that **the education of my student is primarily my responsibility.** However, as a member of the TCA community, TCA makes the following commitments to my family:

TCA's commitment to you:

- The TCA staff is committed to assisting my family in developing my student into an exemplary citizen within the parameters of the TCA mission statement;

- The TCA staff acknowledges that their relationship with me is a partnership and frequent communication is an essential component of that relationship;

- The TCA staff will do their best not to undermine the values of my family;

- The TCA staff commits to uphold the philosophical foundation and core values listed on the TCA Web site, such as:

- Small class sizes (typically a maximum of 20 students);

- Character education based on traditional American values;

- Interactive and hands-on teaching methods, consistent with the Charlotte Mason principles, the trivium, and the Socratic Method;

- Consistent scope and sequence curriculum;

- Comprehensive phonics, literature and math;

- Classical subjects including logic, rhetoric, and Latin;

- All students studying foreign language beginning in kindergarten;

- Fine Arts and Physical Education;

- Dynamic, dedicated, and carefully screened teachers and staff (whether or not they possess Colorado licensure);

- Homework that fosters a passion for learning and facilitates the development of well-rounded students;

- Half-day kindergarten (in order to limit school time for very young children).

By signing this Letter of Understanding, I acknowledge that my family is committing to TCA and that TCA is committing to my family. I understand that this is not a legally binding document for my family or TCA, but does represent an understanding of the information presented above.

Parent Signature Date

_____

Student (grades 7th-12th) Signature Date

_____

Principal Signature Date

_____ CENTRAL / EAST / NORTH

Student's CLEARLY PRINTED NAME CAMPUS LOCATION CURRENT OR ENTERING GRADE

For more information about The Classical Academy, please visit www.tcad20.org.

Ask the charter schools you are interested in to provide you with its written expectations. Sometimes you may find this in the charter school's parent handbook, which may even be available on the Internet.

CHAPTER 10
Curricula

What curriculum is used in charter schools?

That's a narrow question that deserves a broad answer. It's like asking, "Which kind of car is driven on U.S. roads?"

There is a multitude of curricula used in charter schools, and autonomy from the public districts creates a greater freedom in choosing and implementing learning programs. This is a huge perk for teachers, administrators—and especially the students—since school professionals have the power to tweak and torque the curricula to fit the students.

Some national charter models may actually be designed around a certain curriculum such as Core Knowledge, Expeditionary Learning, and Montessori, while others charters may design their own curriculum, or use a combination of techniques within the school.

While you need to inquire with the charter school you are considering about their chosen academics courses, we can briefly describe some popular charter school learning programs.

Core Knowledge

This wildly popular curriculum is not only used in charter schools, but in many different school settings. The Core Knowledge curriculum is based on research of some of the highest performing elementary schools around the world, and collaborative input from parents, scientists, and academic professionals. It is a curriculum based on sequenced learning, meaning that knowledge is built on knowledge.

The Core Knowledge Foundation was founded in 1986 by educator and academic critic E.D. Hirsch, Jr. He wrote the book *Cultural Literacy: What Every American Needs to Know* in 1987. What Americans needed to know was a lot. Ten years later Hirsch published *The Schools We Need and Why We Don't Have Them*. It was the following year that he started releasing Core

Knowledge books in a series, which focused on content knowledge that should be taught at particular elementary grade levels.

For more information visit www.coreknowledge.org.

Examples of Core Knowledge Charter Schools:
  Verona Area Charter School (WI)
  West Houston Charter School (TX)
  Charleston Development Academy Charter (SC)

Expeditionary Learning

Expeditionary Learning was developed by Outward Bound USA, and founded on the ideas of Outward Bound's creator, Kurt Hahn. The program has an emphasis on student character and academics. The educational model is composed of "learning expeditions," which describes an experience of a theme or question as a building element. The students learn subjects through service to others, adventures, and fieldwork research. Expeditionary Learning has developed several books on its educational approach. Emily Cousins edited *Roots, from Outward Bound to Expeditionary Learning* and authored *Reflections on Design Principles*. Also available is *Core Practices and Benchmarks,* which is available in both English and Spanish.

Program description by ELS:

"Now in its sixteenth year, Expeditionary Learning Schools (ELS) helps create and improve public schools by bettering student achievement, building student character, and enhancing teacher practice. The Expeditionary Learning School network serves over 140 schools in 28 states and the District of Columbia, supporting 40,000 students and 4,300 teachers. Expeditionary Learning is supported by schools, school districts, and grants. Expeditionary Learning schools thrive from a community commitment to each student's academic and character growth; from active hands-on, twenty-first century teaching and learning; a school culture valuing nature, adventure, and personal challenge; and from an uncommonly extensive and highly regarded teacher professional development program.

The ELS approach is experiential and project-based, involving students in original research with experts to create high-quality products for audiences beyond the classroom.

ELS is a comprehensive school reform nonprofit with roots in Outward Bound and the belief that students can be encouraged to achieve more than they ever thought possible. EL schools offer compelling testimony that school success can both include and mean more than high test scores."

—*Expeditionary Learning Schools Outward Bound*

Examples of ELS charter schools:
    Lighthouse Community Charter School (CA)
    Russell Byers Charter School (PA)
    Genesee Community Charter School (NY)

Montessori

The International Montessori Index explains, "Montessori is not a system for training children in academic studies, nor is it a label to be put on educational materials. It is a method of observing and supporting the natural development of children." The Montessori educational approach was founded by Dr. Maria Montessori, who was Italy's first female physician. She dedicated herself to scientific observation of children's learning processes. Dr Montessori used this research to prepare an environment in which a child learns by choosing learning activities. Montessori practices in the classroom are seldom in the form of group lessons led by an adult; instead they focus around individual choice of research and work.

There is a multitude of literature and curricula designed around the Montessori method by various authors, available online and in bookstores.

To learn more about Montessori and materials available, visit amshq.org.

Examples of Montessori Charter Schools:
    East Cooper Montessori Charter School (SC)
    Keystone Montessori Charter School (AZ)
    Chinook Montessori Charter School (AK)

College Preparatory and Early College

Some charter high schools are designed to go beyond a high school diploma. These courses are often referred to as college preparatory. Charter schools with this specialty groom college-ready kids by teaching university-level expectations and organization.

Classes may be taught in a lecture hall format to familiarize students with such a learning environment, as well as teach study habits that will equip them for future academic success. College prep high schools exist in all ranges of demographic areas. There are charters that are geared toward inner-city students who may be the first generation to attend college, and there are schools that target intellectual risk-takers who seek serious academics and accelerated courses. College preparatory schools may offer college credits to students, whereas early college high schools commonly provide opportunities for a student to earn an associate's degree as part of the high school program.

Not only does this approach set students up on an academically rigorous path into college, but it's also a taxpayer's and parent's dream. Since charter schools are tuition free and many of these college course offerings too, a taxpaying citizen would not only send these students through high school, but into college as well, meaning no tuition costs for the parents while the child is enrolled in high school. The extra education for college preparatory and early college kids cost the same money as funding the neighborhood school, but can save parents a bundle and trim time off future college for students. The correct term for this twofold learning system is "dual enrollment." Since I am a bargain-hunting, coupon-cuttin', blue-light special kind of mom—the cost efficiency alone of this schooling approach makes me a fan.

Examples of early college charter schools:
   Colorado Springs Early Colleges (CO)
   YES Prep Public School (TX)
   Gateway to College (GA)
   Effie Kokrine Charter School (AK)

Program description by YES Prep Public Schools:
"YES Prep Public Schools exist to increase the number of low-income Houstonians who graduate from a four-year college prepared to compete in

the global marketplace and committed to improving disadvantaged communities.

- YES has 1 college counselor per 25 students. In a public Houston class room today only 10% of sixth graders will graduate from college.

- YES Prep exists to change these odds. And it's working 84% of YES Prep alum has graduated or is still enrolled in college.

- Students cannot earn a high school degree from YES Prep unless they are accepted into a four-year college.

YES has been ranked as the best public school in Houston by *Newsweek, U.S. News & World Report* and the *Houston Chronicle*. For the eighth consecutive year, 100% of YES Prep's graduating seniors have been accepted into four-year colleges, including Harvard, Yale, Columbia, Rice, and Stanford. YES Prep combines a highly successful 6th-12th -grade model along with high standards for student achievement and parental involvement. For more information on YES Prep Public schools www.yesprep.org." *Prep Public Schools (TX)*

Classical Education and Paideia

Much of what is now used in modern education was developed by the western classical education theory. It is focused around three phases of human development, which is then coordinated with student development. This pattern is sometimes describes as "the trivium."

The trivium equals three stages: Primary education, which is the foundation of learning, secondary education which develops the skills, and tertiary education to prepare the person for a profession. In the K-12 charter environment classical education would mean that elementary years are spent teaching the students how to learn and basic knowledge that all other learning requires (such as reading, writing, and math). The middle school years develop critical thinking skills and learning to reason through an argument. High school is when students learn rhetoric and various forms of expression. Classical education focuses on education as known in the middle ages with an influence of ancient Greece and the Paideia concept.

Paideia is also the name of a curriculum written by Robert Hutchins and Mortimer Adler based on this concept. To learn more about Paideia, visit www.paideia.org.

Examples of Classical and Paideia charter schools:
    South Bronx Classical Charter School (NY)
    The Benjamin Franklin Classical Charter Public School (MA)
    Paideia Academy (MN)

Program description by The Classical Academy (TCA)

"The Classical Academy exists to assist parents in their mission to develop exemplary young citizens with superior academic preparation, equipped with analytical thinking skills, a passion for learning, and virtuous character, all built upon a solid foundation of knowledge. TCA's classical approach to education has three significant features. First, teachers utilize hands-on activities and encourage observation and narration. This actively involves the student in the learning process. Second, TCA incorporates the Socratic method and uses a seminar format in the high school years. This creates an interactive and passionate environment, which ignites a love of learning. Finally, TCA follows the classic trivium of education (content, logic, expression) as described by Dorothy Sayers in her essay *The Lost Tools of Learning*. By employing the classical approach, students are better prepared for higher education, are able to cope successfully with the difficulties of a changing society, and are lifelong learners."—*The Classical Academy (CO) has more than 2,600 students and more than 6,000 enrollment hopefuls on the waiting list.*

Science, Technology, Engineering, and Math (STEM)

More and more schools are offering complete education in the sciences. In an era of technology it is pertinent that our children learn to develop skills in this area to become competitive in future professional markets. As one STEM charter founder said, "It is as important for the students to learn to use a computer as it is a pencil. These are the communication tools of the future."

Since sciences and technologies are rapidly evolving, STEM programs should be fluid and adapting. Many charters create their own STEM curricula, or look to organizations such as NASA for input.

Examples of STEM charter schools:
    eSTEM Elementary Public Charter School (AR)
    American Academy (CO)
    Wiseburn Charter School (CA)

Program description by American Academy:

"The American Academy education model is unique and includes programming specifically designed to respond to the "STEM Crisis," which reports that American students are not performing as well in science and math as their international peers (Trends in International Mathematics and Science Study, 2003). The goals of the school include giving students the incentives and skills to pursue higher education in science and high technology in the hopes that these students will be able to compete for desirable STEM jobs in an increasingly international and educated job market.

Our school boasts four science labs—a geoscience and astronomy lab for sixth grade, a life science lab for seventh grade, a chemistry and physical science lab for eighth grade, and an elementary science lab for grades one through five. In addition to the science labs, the American Academy also dedicates space to a STEM lab where a comprehensive STEM curriculum is implemented for all students, beginning in kindergarten. Students study topics such as satellites, forensics, aeronautics, archaeology, and architecture. The engineering design process is practiced in all grades; some of the fields explored include chemical engineering, geotechnical engineering, acoustical engineering, and bioengineering. In middle school, students are exposed to learning through simulations. Through these simulations students engage in virtual space missions and disaster-preparedness exercises. Eighth grade students learn *Satellite Tool Kit* (STK) software where they build scenarios of complex and dynamic real-world problems involving communications and satellites."—*American Academy (Colorado) on the development of its school's custom STEM curricula*

Entrepreneurship

Another growing trend among charter schools is to teach business skills. These schools express a desire to prepare students with skills important in creating and operating their own business ventures. Curricula vary but tend to be inclusive of problem solving, innovation, and creativity in addition to the more traditional textbook learning commonly found in other schools.

These business-focused schools may also offer lessons in financial planning, marketing, business analysis, business plan writing, customer service, and the value of investment.

Examples of entrepreneurship charter schools:
    Ivy Academia (CA)
    Denver Venture School (CO)
    Young Entrepreneurial Vocational Academy (SC)
    Entrepreneurship Preparatory School (OH)

Program description by Cleveland Entrepreneurship Preparatory School:

"Entrepreneurship Preparatory School is successful because of these best practices, which are also used at many of the other successful urban charter schools:

- Extended school day and extended school year

- Culture of high expectations and a "no excuses" approach to education

- Enforced code of conduct and enforced uniform policy

- Mandatory tutoring for students not meeting academic benchmarks

- Zealous teachers who believe that every child can learn and are committed to helping them; a strong presence of teamwork among staff

- Weekly, collaborative professional development for teachers

- Frequent (monthly) academic assessment of students and responsive adjustment to educational plan

- A set of common instructional strategies used across the curriculum, in every classroom

E Prep is unique because of its focus on entrepreneurship. The school was founded by an entrepreneur (John Zitzner) and an educator (Marshall Emerson). Both believe that students are best served if they are taught to see their obstacles as opportunities and to show persistence in the pursuit of their goals. E Prep maintains a focus on these keys to success, which are also keys to entrepreneurial success: courage, self-discipline, respect, responsibility, and perseverance.

E Prep teaches an entrepreneurship class to all of its students. Using the curriculum of the Network for Teaching Entrepreneurship (www.nfte.com), students are taught to identify a business opportunity, how to write a business plan, and how to start and operate a small business. The curriculum demonstrates how academics (especially math) are relevant to real life."

—*Cleveland Entrepreneurship Preparatory School (OH) about their unique program*

CHAPTER 11

Character Development

"The function of education is to teach one to think intensively and to think critically... Intelligence plus character – that is the goal of true education."
—*Martin Luther King, Jr. (1929-1968) civil rights leader*

The curricula chapter is hopelessly incomplete without covering the topic of character development. As a matter of fact, most organizations I contacted for information about their school's curricula forwarded information about their ethics and virtues programs.

A key difference between education and good education is that in addition to learning skills, a good education also teaches students to discern proper ways of using such knowledge. If we only educate our children with facts, but not equip them with problem-solving abilities, or the sense of right and wrong—what will our world look like for future generations?

Some will argue that character comes from within and not something that is learned. That may be true to some extent, but not entirely. Much of a child's behavior and attitude is learned by example. Consider what would happen if you put a plate of *four* warm cookies in front of *five* preschoolers. Most likely the four fastest kids would help themselves to one of the cookies, while the fifth would be left with a quivering bottom lip.

Does that mean that all four of these cookie-eating youngsters are ill-natured? No, it means that although they possessed the knowledge of what a cookie is and the skill to serve oneself—they lacked the foresight of what would result from their actions.

What about teenagers? Sure, the middle and high school years were magical in the egotistical sense for most of us, but should we accept that as an excuse for rudeness and selfishness?

"Precociousness is not a flattering term for teenagers," a teacher recently wrote. He's right. A punk attitude may be age appropriate for a teen, but not addressing the issues would be like not dealing with the toddler who demands ice cream for dinner every night. The kids grow bigger and so do unattended problems. By the same token, if a child has been taught values and how to apply them, then these skills grow with them, too.

If you have any questions about why instilling good character into our students is important, ask your child's history teacher. He or she does not need to go back far in time to tell you about acts of terror, war, and sneaky decisions made by brilliant leaders, which had terrible affects on our world. If history is not enough of a selling point, use this morning's newspaper headlines for inspiration. Corruption and scandals top the front page. Yuck!

This is not the world we want to hand off to our children and grandchildren, and we don't need to. The best way to assure a better place for the next generation is to give the knowledge required for being proper stewards, and this puts character education at the top of the must-know list.

In the charter school world it is not only the student who is educated in virtues, but often the teachers and staff as well. The reason isn't because charter teachers are lacking in the area of personal morals, but quite contrary: they appreciate the importance of the topic and value learning developing information.

As with nearly every topic, not all charter schools feel that character education should be taught in school. Some charters leave ethics and morals for families to cover at home. There are families that feel strongly that this is something they would rather home educate. If this is the case, discuss the topic with your school administrator.

The terms used to describe ethics-based learning at charter schools vary. There are programs referred to as "pillars," "core virtues, "school credo," and simply "character development."

Here are some quotes from well-known organizations:

Description by Our World Neighborhood Foundation (OWN): "The Ten Pillars of a positive community: respect, courage, kindness, friendship, truth, responsibility, self-Discipline, fairness, citizenship, and perseverance. The Pillars of a Positive Community reflect OWN's commitment to social justice. They play an important part in building and supporting our school culture. The Pillars of a Positive Community are a unifying element for the entire school; by the time students enter the middle school, they have been focusing on these ten concepts for many years." —*Our World Neighborhood Foundation, an organization specializing in helping charters to reach ultimate potential and become community-based, self-managed institutions.*

"From kindergarten to the great universities, increased attention is being paid to the proper place of character formation in education. Much energy and resources are going into helping educators find useful tools for implementing character education.

This movement is proceeding in public, private, parochial, and home schools. However, charter schools offer a special opportunity for innovation in this area. Because they are schools of choice, charter schools can engage in moral instruction that might ignite controversy in conventional government schools." —Character Education: Another Niche for Charter Schools, by Robert Holland

"Washington Latin Public Charter School in the District of Columbia, founded in 2006, provides a challenging, classical education that is accessible to students throughout the nation's capital. This school began with grades five through seven and will, by adding a grade each year, eventually have a full high school. All students study Latin, as well as French or Chinese as they get older, and the school's literature-based curriculum ensures a strong background in reading, writing, and public speaking. Washington Latin is college preparatory, but its motto 'Discite, Servaturi,' (Learn, those who are about to serve) emphasizes preparation for effective citizenship.

In its effort to instill strong values of respect, kindness, and compassion, the school regularly and purposefully reminds students that *words matter*. Head of School, Martha Cutts, explains: 'Too often young people use language carelessly. They say things that are unkind and hurtful and later explain that they were just kidding. At WLPCS teachers can point to the *words matter* signs in each classroom and remind students that how one uses language does make a difference.'" —*Washington Latin Public Charter School, Washington DC*

CHAPTER 12
Homework

"I was wondering if the charter school really was as far ahead as people were saying. But after the first week's homework I was convinced it was true," said one mother of a recent charter school student.

This type of reaction is not uncommon. When a charter school is academically rigorous the amount and content of the homework reflects it.

I can personally attest to the difference in homework as I have had children in both traditional and charter schools. For example, my child who attended kindergarten in the neighborhood school had homework inconsistently, and it was very basic. I actually embarrassed myself by calling the teacher five months into the school year to ask if the kids were going to have math homework at this grade level. The teacher replied that my son had been doing math homework since week one. After probing I realized that worksheets asking, "Which drawer is on the bottom?" and "Circle the elephant in the middle," were considered math.

My children who attended the rigorous charter school had daily homework, which consisted of reading ten minutes with your child, spelling, and math (counting, adding, and subtracting). The children were using first grade books by the second month in Kindergarten.

Is one better than the other? That's a question each parent needs to decide. The better question is whether one is a better fit for your child.

Also, do not assume that an increase in homework is to be expected with every charter school. It is important that you ask the policy guidelines of the school you are considering. Here is a sample homework policy:

"Homework is an integral part of the education program at our charter school. What we learn at school is reinforced by learning at home. Homework fosters skills and concepts that are taught and helps develop good study skills and habits. It also communicates to parents of what is being taught in the classroom. Here are guidelines for the assignments:

- Homework should be assigned by the teachers daily, but exceptions may be made by said teacher.

- Teachers are expected to assign certain homework, evaluate and differentiate them as much as possible to the student's ability, and relate them to the course mission. Should a student consistently not complete homework within the suggested time, the teacher should be contacted. The same applies if the student consistently finishes homework too quickly.

- Here is the suggested minimum time a student should spend on homework:

    Kindergarten: 30 minutes (incl. 15 min. reading)

    Lower elementary grades: 30-45 minutes (incl.20 min. reading)

    Upper elementary grades: 40-60 minutes

    Middle school: 1 hour plus

    - **Make-up Work for Excused Absences only**
    Make-up work assignments will be provided when *the student returns from the absence.* Each day of excused absence equals two days to make up work. All work must be submitted in a timely fashion, and teachers will provide the due date for each assignment. Work which was assigned prior to absence is due the first day the student returns to school. **Unexcused absences do not warrant make-up work**

    - **Late Work**
    Elementary Grades: Student receives one lower letter grade on tardy homework. The teacher may use discretion to permit the child another opportunity in completing the assignment in timely manner for partial credit. If late homework is a frequent occurrence the teacher may schedule a conference with both the student and parent.

Middle school: Each teacher uses his/her discretion as to whether late work will be accepted and graded."

The above is a sample from one school. As mentioned, homework policies vary greatly. The same goes for attendance rules. Some charter schools offer flexibility with attendance at the school building, particularly if it is a distance learning or online program. Others may have firmer rules. One of the urban charter schools interviewed has in their written policy that ten days missed in one school year equals an automatic repeat of the school year. The reason given is that too many days missed creates too much pressure on the student to catch up. The mission of this particular school is to close the achievement gap, graduate an educated student, and prepare the child for a vocation or a college of interest.

CHAPTER 13

ESL, GT, and SPED

"You can pick your friends, you can pick your seat, but you cannot pick your friend's seat. These were some of the fundamental rules we learned as preschoolers. As amusing as it sounds, we can apply these same guiding principles to our public charter schools." —*Charter School Speed with SPED, 2008 Blog www.yourhub.com* "How Swede it is"

Have you ever heard someone say that charter schools test better because they do not accept special-needs students? Next time you can tell them they are incorrect.

Charter schools must answer to the same antidiscrimination laws as district schools and cannot turn away a child due to academic needs. Families, however, may choose not to accept enrollment in a charter school if they feel this particular school is not the best environment for their student.

What is a special needs student? To clarify the matter I searched definitions of special education on the trusty Internet. This is what www.answers.com had to say:

> "Special education [n] classrooms or private instruction involving techniques, exercises, and subject matter designed for students whose learning needs cannot be met by a standard school curriculum."

The range of special needs is broad and includes handicaps, learning disorders, and language barriers. More and more people are also grouping gifted and talented education into the special- needs category as this learning level may also not be offered within the standard school curriculum.

Public schools must answer to both state and federal laws about offering adequate special education (SPED). In other words, it is unlawful not to provide adequate special learning services for a child who requires it. Some charter authorizers mandate the charters to subscribe to district services to assure liability and quality control, whereas other authorizers permit the charters to purchase SPED services through alternate venues.

Charter schools may also offer more individual attention to all students due to program design and smaller class sizes. The freedom to explore beyond the boundaries of curricula is another advantage.

A few years back I volunteered at a brand-new charter school. Budgets and resources were tight as the goal was to move out of the barracks and construct a permanent building on the opposite end of the lot. I was early and walked in at the tail end of math class. Three classes were occupied with the first graders actively working. The kids had been divided into groups and the math levels were across the board. Some of the kids were working on addition and subtraction, whereas another group was doing three-digit multiplication. It was amazing to watch the teacher's teamwork between the classrooms.

One boy was wearing a four-foot long plush snake around his neck with both ends skimming the floor beneath his desk. At a closer look I realized it was the same child who just last week had had trouble keeping his entire person in his own space. This time he was sitting in his seat working by himself (and on his own paper)! The teacher must have caught me watching him.

"My own son had sensory issues and ADD growing up," she said. "Our pediatrician asked us to use a toy snake similar to that one to help my son feel 'weighted.' It worked well for my child, so I asked the parents if we could try it with Nolan (not his real name)."

Last week I ran into the same boy at a very rigorous academic charter middle school.

There was no plush snake around his neck. Instead he had a messenger bag slung around his shoulders and a soccer ball in his arms. Little known to him, he will always remind me of the ways some of our charter school teachers creatively work with the needs of each student in their class without the formal label.

Charter schools are also growing as a quality options for children with specific challenges.

Colorado recently approved three charter schools specifically for autistic children. These types of charters have been around for a while and serving children whose needs are beyond what an ordinary classroom may offer.

The New York Center for Autism Charter School was the first of schools in New York solely dedicated for children with autism spectrum disorder (ASD). The program is housed within one of the PS 50 school buildings and has seven classrooms for its twenty-eight students. The teacher to student ratio is 1:1. Since the charter school is located inside a "regular" public school, there are plenty of opportunities for the NYCA Charter School students to socialize, while learning takes place in an environment designed for the developing student. NYCA Charter School is a nongraded school, meaning that the children graduate when they have the requirements, not after finishing a certain grade level.

While NYCA Charter School originated as a charter school, this is not always the case for all charters. Princeton House Charter School (FL), a program for children with autism, was founded by three mothers and started off as a private school in one of their homes. The first year of operating, the private school had six students enrolled. The program quickly gained a reputation as the leader within its field and was recognized nationally for its "best practices" in serving children on the autism spectrum. Just two short years later Princeton House converted to a public charter school as a means of reaching more children and offering a program free of private school tuition. As of 2009, Princeton House Academy serves 230 children ages three to twenty. The goal is to provide early intervention focusing on acquisition skills in language, social skills, and behavior modifications, as well as preparing the students for a life after school. Life skills are taught as a key component of the Princeton House program and the school has partnered with local businesses in developing employment knowledge. When it comes to special needs, charter autonomy is the perfect environment for exploration and implementation of cutting edge tools and research.

Kristen Smith, the assistant director for Front Range Academy (multiple Colorado learning centers for HOPE Online Learning Academy Co-op) says, "There is no such thing as a learning disability. There are only teaching disabilities. Everyone can learn." When asked to define the term at-risk, Kristen replies, "Every student is at risk of either failing or succeeding. 'At risk' means much more than socioeconomics."

Front Range Academy is known to attract students who have been identified as "at risk" of academic failure or dropping out. The range of kids, personalities, and abilities that attends these centers as well as other HOPE co-op academies is broad and more a reflection of local demographics than family income and skin tone.

Alcohol and substance abuse programs are not necessarily considered learning components, but offered by many charter schools. Another charter school director emotionally explained that she had just been meeting with a student, who had come to her for help for his addiction. "We're a family," she said. "We are here for these kids to help them be successful in life. When a kid trusts the adults with their problems, whether it is academically related or not, it is a sign that the school is doing great things. At school we teach academics, but we also teach trust, respect, compassion, and partnership."

Charter schools are well known for being effective tools for closing academic achievement gaps, and taking on some of the more difficult students that were not progressing in the broader system. Charter schools like KIPP, SEED, and many others specifically set out to reach these particular demographics of kids. Recent studies also show that students from charter schools are more likely to go to college and less likely to drop out of college programs.

Then we have the topic of English as a Second Language (ESL). I was an ESL student in high school. Granted I did not go to a charter school, but it was a public school nevertheless. My first language was Swedish and I must say I have never run into a Swedish speaking ESL teacher as long as I was a student. I'm sure they exist, just not in abundance in the area I lived in. Instead I learned English in a shared classroom of multilingual classmates from across our globe. If you had Spanish or Filipino as a main language, there was likely someone who could translate, otherwise we found alternative methods of figuring it out.

Charter schools often deal with similar situations. Many schools may be able to offer specially designated teachers who are fluent in more commonly shared languages, otherwise resources may be shared from the district if available. However, there are charter schools that specialize in languages and offer cultural immersion programs. Languages like Spanish, Chinese, Mandarin, French, Japanese, Latin, and so on may be the very mission or focus of these schools. The small school environment offered at many charters may also foster close-knit relationships between other students and staff to also help kids along who are not fluent in English.

You know your child better than anyone and should decide if immersing your child in his current first language is a better learning environment, rather than immersing him in English. My personal experience as someone who has gone through the shift of first languages was that years of textbook English did not teach me as efficiently as having to use the language on an everyday basis. But this is not me; it is your child. If you feel hesitant about which approach and program is better for him, consult professionals within the field and talk to the schools you are considering.

Regardless of the source of a school's special education, English as a second language, or gifted and talented—there is always more that can be done.

"No" and "cannot" should not apply toward a child's needs. Instead, we need to continue to ask ourselves what else we can do to make our education programming better. Research within this field will continue to unmask methods as to how we can better equip our schools in supporting students who have needs beyond standard classroom offerings. Some of these findings may be challenging to provide due to financing and other obstacles. However, we are charter families. We choose to diversify our children's public education by seeking possibilities. Partner with your school in pursuit of seeking solutions and funding (grants, donations, and legislative changes). You will be amazed at the mountains that can be moved by a few dedicated families. It is the type of impact that will not only benefit your child, but also many others.

For additional information about special education, ESL, and gifted and talented programming for your state, contact your state education office (information in the index).

"Hi! My name is Jordan and I am nine. I go to North Star Academy. My favorite thing is animals so when I grow up, I want to be a veterinarian. I am special because I have Asperger's and sensory issues. My old school didn't help me. I could not read or focus and I felt lost and confused. My charter school is great because everyone helps me.

Teachers help me with reading and spelling and give me extra attention. Shurley English and phonics have helped me jump two grade levels in reading in one year. Reading is important to veterinarians to find out which medicines animals need. Parents volunteer because they love their kids' school. They help so the teacher can work with other kids and grade tests. My principal is kind and special. She teaches Character Education. She teaches us about integrity, justice, freedom, and especially how to be respectful. This will help me be a kind vet.

At my old school I didn't believe I could be anything. Now I earn academic and good behavior medals. All the people at North Star are helping me grow up to be whatever I want to be, especially a veterinarian."

—*Jordan Rae Rowley, a third grader at North Star Academy (Parker, Colorado), the elementary school winner of the Colorado League of Charter Schools (the League), and College Invest 2009 Charter School Essay Contest.*

JORDAN ROWLEY'S PARENTS ON JORDAN'S AWARD WINNING ESSAY

Jordan's greatest challenge with the essay contest was staying within the word limit—she had so many more great things she wanted to write about her experience at her charter school! That said, for us, it wasn't Jordan's winning the contest that meant so much but rather what she wrote. As her parents, we of course feel an immense sense of pride in her accomplishment. More importantly, though, with her heartfelt two hundred words, she validated so many of the actions we've taken on her behalf, especially the move to North Star Academy two years ago.

Over the past few years we've learned a great deal about the challenges a twice-exceptional student presents. Due to their higher intellect, these children often unwittingly mask their learning disabilities. We always believed that we'd find the right combination of diagnosis, therapies, and understanding to bring out the best in Jordan. We hadn't imagined what an enormous role her charter school would play.

When we toured NSA the very first time, the assistant principal casually mentioned that if a child needs extra help, NSA doesn't wait for testing and documentation; rather, they immediately begin working to give the student the help he or she needs. At that point he had no idea that we had a child who needed extra help and we were just completing a year of struggling with the neighborhood school where they made it nearly impossible to get her the help she needed. We lived the horror story of bureaucracy, incompetence, and total lack of regard by the administrators and psychological service personnel in that school. We finally got Jordan on a limited Individual Education Plan (IEP) during the last week of the school year. Needless to say, we were sold on our charter school at that first visit.

Admittedly, when we first began investigating charter schools we didn't know how the selection process worked. What we did know was that Jordan had a frustrating year in a private kindergarten class and a miserable first grade experience at the local public school. Since it was clear to us that the neighborhood school was willing to let her fall through the cracks, we knew that we had to find a way to get her out of that system. Finding NSA, discovering that everyone has a chance at enrollment, and being fortunate enough to get in was life changing for our family.

Over the last couple of years we've heard the handpicking accusation suffered by many charter schools. Jordan's challenges are not always obvious. People usually comment on how bright she is and assume that is why she was selected for NSA. In these discussions we don't necessarily mention her learning disabilities, but we do make it a point to educate others on how the selection process really works. We're also quick to add our own personal sound bite that we hope sticks with them, "Charter schools don't pick the best students—they bring out the best in students." That's certainly proven to be the case with Jordan, and her winning the Colorado League of Charter Schools essay contest is a strong testament to that.

Some things may never come easily for Jordan, but we do feel that by having her in this charter school, full of caring teachers, concerned administrators, and involved parents, so much is falling into place for Jordan that we no longer fear her falling through the cracks.

—*Michelle D. Carlisle and Sheila R. Rowley, parents of Jordan Rowley, North Star Academy (CO)*

Robert's story

Chris Behnke is a passionate mom. You can hear the strength in her words when she speaks of the journey of her son—Robert.

Robert was born with mild Down's syndrome, hypotonic, deafness, and later in life he was diagnosed with Dyslexia and ADD.

During Robert's early years, the Behnkes lived in San Diego, California. One of the few sounds Robert could hear was the vacuum cleaner, which frightened him so much his mother would ask a neighbor to watch him during housecleaning. The neighbor would bring little Robert with her to her prayer group where they would jointly pray for the child and his family.

The Behnkes dedicated themselves to Robert's care and condition and quickly had the toddler in an infant program, which specialized in speech, muscle training, and sign language. When Robert was about three years old, the family moved to Colorado. After four years of schooling, something remarkable happened—Robert was no longer deaf. Call it delayed development, or proper therapy, but Chris is not shy in who she is crediting for the child's healing—God.

This was certainly not the end for Robert's challenges ahead. The local school where Robert was enrolled could only meet limited needs for strengthening therapy services, mostly in form of PE classes.

After trying five different schools and still seeking the best fit in schooling for Robert, the Behnkes enrolled him in a famed Colorado charter school, Ridgeview Classical School.

Chris was well aware of the school's reputation for accelerated and rigorous academics, but she was desperate in finding a solution for Robert's academic needs. Although skeptical that a school could meet the now seventh grader's unique combination of special needs, she accepted the charter school placement for her child. After all, Ridgeview Classical is known for its high parent satisfaction ratings.

A few months into seventh grade, Chris was growing increasingly anxious that the new school experience would not bring a difference to her son. Fueled by years of frustration, she marched into the school office and bluntly laid out her concerns to the school leadership. This tactic had not yielded much change in the other schools, but much to Chris' surprise, her voice as a worried mother was finally heard.

A plan was created for Robert, which included student services and adjusting his grade level to where he could progress successfully. The Behnkes formed a partnership with the school leadership in growing Robert's education based on *his* needs.

"Robert should be graduating next year," Chris writes. "Instead he will be entering high school. My son, however, has now got the ability to write a decent thesis paper and do better in his classes. He won a silver medal for the National Mythology Exam last year in his Latin class and was one point away from the gold. I am so proud of him and proud of my school."

Chris Behnke is crossing her fingers for one more high school achievement for Robert—he is on track to be the valedictorian of his graduating class.

"The Infinity Charter School is located in Harrisburg, Pennsylvania, and was chartered in 2003. The school is designed to meet the intellectual, academic, and social-emotional needs of mentally gifted children, and was founded by Ms. Nancy J. Hall, based on a similar charter school she developed and operated near Denver, Colorado (1994 – 1999). ICS has been re-chartered through 2012.

Research indicates that mentally gifted children have abilities that require special services that are not ordinarily met in the regular classroom or through limited pullout programs. In addition, evidence indicates that these children represent one of the most unidentified and underserved populations of special-need students in regular public school systems. At ICS, specially trained teachers provide full-time educational programming tailored to meet the special needs of these underserved children.

While it is commonly assumed that the gifted will 'make it on their own,' it is a well- documented fact that these students are often significantly 'at risk.' Without an education that appropriately addresses their intellectual, academic, and social-emotional needs, these children are at risk for underachievement, dropping out, doing drugs, turning to delinquency, and even committing suicide. This is not only a tragic waste of individual potential, but constitutes a significant loss for the community and nation as well.

The educational components of the school have been selected based on educational research and/or a survey of best practices. In particular, ICS offers a number of unique programming elements, including yearlong, integrated themes in science and social studies, as well as individualized spelling and math programs. Most are specifically designed to address the particular characteristics and needs of intellectually and/or academically gifted children, while others are appropriate for all children—but all, we believe, are beneficial for our students.

ICS does not have (by law) admission criteria and the school is open to all who feel the school meets the needs of their children. Admission to the school is by an annual lottery, and each year, ICS has a waiting list of approximately forty to fifty students. ICS currently serves approximately 120 students, but the school's board is actively exploring the development and construction of a new facility that will allow the school to expand to 320 students, in grades K-8."—*The Infinity Charter School (PA)*

"Ashley, a senior at Hope Online's New Heights Academy, overcame what she had come to believe was her destiny. While this would normally be a contradiction in terms, New Heights Academy Learning Director, Denise Duran, insists that, in Ashley's case, it is not. Her remarkable turnaround reminds us that the proverbial cards life deals us, *can* be shuffled and re-dealt with the right support and a powerful vision of change.

Ms. Duran seized the opportunity three years ago to provide that vision for Ashley. After a bumpy start, including weeks of negative remarks during classes, Ms. Duran offered her new student a choice. 'You can do this the easy way or the hard way,' Ms. Duran recalls having told Ashley. 'You can prove that everyone expecting you to fail is wrong and that you are capable, strong, and smart. Or, you can do it the hard way, by being negative and giving in to your difficult circumstances. It's your choice.'

For Ashley, this meant 'digging deep' and finding the faith to believe her new mentor. It meant forging ahead despite several serious strikes against her. Then just a freshman, Ashley had arrived at New Heights Academy on probation and with a network of friends who did not value education. Her one glimmer of academic inspiration had just been snuffed out when her older sister's college scholarship opportunities dissolved with a teen pregnancy. Understandably, academic failure seemed inevitable.

'If her older sister, whom many considered academically gifted, could not succeed in school, then Ashley had no confidence to believe that she could,' shares Ms. Duran. 'It took the proof from assessments to help Ashley distinguish between the 'cannot' and 'will not' factors of her performance. I was able to show her, on paper, that she had measurable skills and knowledge and only needed the individual attention we are able to offer through Hope Online.'

In the last three years, Ashley has proven, to herself and others, that success is now her *chosen* destiny. 'I have gone from a .867 GPA to being a straight A student and I *will* graduate this spring,' she confidently announces. Her relationships at school are now supportive of her academic goals. She thinks and acts more independently and understands the correlation between positive behavior and rewarding outcomes. Along the way, she also became a valued employee. Every shift at work is an opportunity to heed Ms. Duran's advice to honor the qualities attributed to her in job references.

'I am so proud of her,' beams Ms. Duran. 'Our graduates have to apply to three colleges and fill out grant forms as a requirement. Ashley has already selected her top programs in South Carolina and Puerto Rico, and she is setting her own vision for life after graduation."

—HOPE On-line Co-op

"Founded in 1995 with 160 students in grades K to 5, Community of Peace Academy presently serves a diverse Pre-K to12 student population on the east side of St. Paul, MN.

Of nearly 700 students, 83% qualify for free and price-reduced meals, and over 60% are learning English as their second language. The majority are Hmong, recent immigrants from Laos and Thailand. About 32% are African American, Hispanic, and European American.

The vision of this award-winning charter school is to educate the whole person—mind, body, and will. The desired outcome is that graduates will freely make decisions and choices that promote mental, physical, emotional, and spiritual health and well-being, for themselves and others.

To this end, programs and practices are designed to promote a strong sense of belonging within a peaceful, caring, and supportive learning community. The school employs a diverse and highly qualified staff of individuals who are committed to the vision and mission of the school and act as role models for students. Each staff member, student, and parent is treated with unconditional positive regard.

In addition to a rigorous academic program, the school provides meaningful, transformative experiences for all students. Such experiences include the visual and performing arts, athletic programs, field trips, class trips, retreats, and service projects. The Academy Choir has been called the school's 'crown jewel.'

Community of Peace Academy was named a National School of Character in 2003 by the Character Education Partnership in Washington DC, and was one of eight charter schools in America included in a U.S. Department of Education publication entitled, 'Successful Charter Schools' (2004) for demonstrated success over time in boosting student achievement. In 2007 the school was named a National Charter School of the Year by the Center for Education Reform in Washington DC."

—*Community of Peace Academy, St. Paul, MN.*

More information is available in a book written by the founder, Karen J. Rusthoven, Ed.D. (2007), entitled, Success in Education through Peace, Healing, and Hope.

About Megan

"My daughter, Megan, had some challenges early on in school. Her kindergarten teacher, Mrs. Brocka, came to us with some concerns shortly after school started in the fall. Megan had difficulty putting sounds together and was troubled putting the basic building blocks of reading. Later, in first grade, she also transposed the letter letters B and D routinely—a sign of dyslexia. At the start of first grade, it was recommended that she get started with an IEP at school, and start services with the special education department at Platte River Academy. We had several meetings over the course of two years to discuss the best course of action to help Megan be successful in the classroom. We met Diane Swan at the first of these meetings and immediately liked her. She and the entire special education department had nothing but Megan's best interest at heart, and came up with many strategies to help her succeed. I can't say enough about Diane's commitment to helping Megan overcome her reading challenge.

On the recommendation of our pediatrician, we had Megan tested at Children's Hospital in January 2009 to see if there was any medication that could help. The specialist diagnosed the same problems that PRA had and in fact told us that Megan is exactly where she needs to be at PRA. She mentioned that the diagnosis and testing Megan has received at PRA goes far and above what she would have received, even in Douglas County. Most public schools, she told us, would not have the intense special education program that Megan has at PRA. We were very pleased and encouraged to receive this news.

All of these services have been coming to fruition just recently; Megan has shown some dramatic improvement in many areas of her academic career, and we feel so blessed to have her in PRA and the special education program there. This is also a testament to her current classroom teachers, Kirsten Halpert and Laurie Knapp; they have both been instrumental in Megan's success this year. We feel especially proud of PRA that they were on top of her challenges as early as kindergarten and started receiving help before it got too difficult to catch up with her peers."

—*Marc & Deb Shupe, Platte River Academy (CO)*

For more information:
    www.newyorkcenterforautism.com
    www.princeton-house.org

CHAPTER 14

Discipline

I still remember my mother declaring the penalty for my childish indiscretions, then ending her statement with these words: "This is harder on me than it is on you."

At the time it made no sense at all. How would *my* lack of attendance at *my* friend's sleepover be harder on my *mother* than myself?

As a mother of three I have found that answer. It is not fun being the heavy. I would much rather be the pal who never has to discipline. More so, I wish that there would never be behavior- deserving punishment. But that is not reality. It is also not realistic to believe that academic rigor, small schools, and parental involvement is a recipe for not needing a stringent disciplinary policy.

Most charter teachers I have spoken with have told me that one of the very reasons they choose to teach at a charter school is because of the strict disciplinary guidelines. A breach in discipline can include forgetting homework, dress code violations, impolite language toward staff and peers, poor choice of actions, and more.

There are times when a disciplinary code has been breached, a student punished, and a parent surprised by how seriously a school deals with infractions. Misconduct should be expected to be dealt with instantly and deliberately. Upon enrolling in a charter school one should receive a handbook of policies and the high standard to which your student will answer.

Wearing mismatched socks in a uniformed school may result in loss of a "dress-down day," forgotten homework may equal missed recess, and rolling one's eyes at the teacher may get the student—and his limber eyeballs—a close-up view of the principal's office.

A school's disciplinary policy is in place to prevent more serious problems. Some charters deal with children who have already been in the juvenile justice system, and one can imagine the types of experiences these kids have had. Other charters are heavily frequented by students with a lot of home support and family ethics. These families urge the schools in reflecting their high standards in disciplinary codes.

Disciplinary codes are designed to provide safety and an orderly environment conducive to learning. These rules will teach the children to become responsible individuals and function in future situations with high behavioral standards.

Keep in mind that spending lunch inside so a student can complete his homework is probably a whole lot harder on the school staff than it is on your child.

CHAPTER 15

Dress Code

Did you think that only parochial schools wear uniform? Think again.

Many public charters have uniforms or specific dress codes. To dress for success is something many schools feel is important to teach the students as they become young adults. In a culture where materialism, pressure from peers, fashion, and pop culture is rampant, we'd be so lucky to have school uniforms.

Sure, a sixteen-year-old who has worn the same plaid since kindergarten will grow tired of limited choice in attire. But a parent who struggles with a child's daily complaint of "I have nothing to wear," would welcome the ability to answer, "You may wear navy or white. Choose one."

Many schools have no-logo rules on clothing and accessories. In other words, you can spend a gazillion dollars on brand-new sneakers, but nobody can tell the difference between those and the discount store shoes when the label is not visible. These rules prevent teasing and pressures for children who may not want—or have the means—to buy "in items."

As a mother of three, I must say I appreciate the money savings school uniforms provide. Sure, it is expensive come July and I preorder the next year's uniforms times three kids. At the same time I realize that I am spending much less by purchasing school-specific attire than taking my kids shopping for what they would like to wear.

And then there are the hand-me-downs. Most charter schools that have strict dress codes subscribe to timeless, classic garments. Collared polos, plaid jumpers, flat-front slacks, and turtle necks may not be on the cover of teen-vogue—but they don't go out of style between kids either. A navy turtleneck looks just as much like a navy turtleneck on this year's third grader as it did two years ago.

Oh, and you may just want to check that handy-dandy charter school handbook on grooming policies, too. There will likely be rules regarding tattoos, piercings, accessories—and yes, haircuts. But as usual, there are as many variances to dress codes as there are charter schools. Some charters don't really pay much attention to whether or not your kid's pants cover his murky boxers, or your daughter is so pierced that her face springs leaks when she drinks from the water fountain. Again, we'll just give you a heads up to check school policy of where you wish to enroll your child.

CHAPTER 16

School Facility

You know that tattered saying "Don't judge a book by its cover?" Well, you really can't judge education by its school building either. There are fabulous buildings that house kids who are not learning and some really lousy buildings that churn out academic excellence by the droves. It's amazing how many families are lured by a pretty façade, convinced this equals qualified staff and education achievement.

Charter school families are usually faced with a choice—academics or amenities (more in chapter 17). To many charter schools a pretty building becomes an amenity.

To date charter school funding is not equal with the district counterpart, and few are the states in which law includes charter schools in building construction funds, such as local bond elections. Therefore most of our nation's charter schools seek facility financing through grants and donations. Sadly this is not always enough to cover such expenses and many charters pay a portion of the school's facilities expenses from the operating revenue. As a result there are a lot of compromises and creativity in finding school facilities to permit the focus to surround academics. After all, isn't that the business schools are in?

If you are entertaining the idea of enrolling your child in a newer charter school, odds are the program is held in a temporary building. This may mean rented space in a shopping center, warehouse district, church—or trailers on a vacant lot.

These facilities are far from glamorous and you often have to overlook the shabby locations to find the schools hidden treasure—a fantastic education.

Many charter school buildings are like chocolate-filled rice cakes. The exterior presentation is bland, flavorless, and lacks personality. If you can get past this you may be rewarded by finding the rich and sweet filling. Permanent school locations are still designed on a shoestring budget, and what many would assume as a normal facility offering may not be so at a charter.

Core subjects and those that meet the charter mission tend to have their own space in a charter building. This means that even a seasoned school may be lacking a school library, PE hall, science room, music room, art room, cafeteria, and kitchen—to mention a few. It does not necessarily mean that the kids don't have access to loaning books, certain subjects, or food. It simply means that the school may be offering crafty solutions that do not require such space.

The tech lab may be a cart on wheels that comes to the home classrooms, the music teacher may share a room with the French teacher, and the public library book mobile may be the provider of loaned literary services.

At my kid's school lunch is served by a catering service in the PE hall, which also doubles as a car pool hall and features a stage for drama performances. The middle school students get shuttled by parent volunteers to a local recreation center for swimming, cycling, and other sports that the school cannot offer on its own.

On that note, we should also mention sports programs. While many charters may provide either school sports or make them available through an outsourced organization, there are some sports more easily offered than others. Let's use football as an example. Having a field is not always the only problem, but school size matters. If a charter has a total of 100 middle school students, all of them are not going to be interested in signing up for the team. My son would add that this is not all bad.

So imagine a football team with seven players. The playbook would pretty much have one play—"go long!" So are football and other team sports out for smaller charters? Of course not! It just means that you have to think outside the yard lines. Some charters pool their kids together with other small charter school kids and form one area team. Others team up with district sports and offer arrangements through the neighborhood schools. Charter schools may even rent out a school-owned field to an outside organization with the agreement to include the school's students on the team.

There are more serious problems as a result of building inadequacies. Some are safety related. The school staff typically goes out of their way to work with landlords and inspection agencies on making sure these problems are dealt with. Some issues are more easily solved than others.

This is also an area where we, the parents, can help. If your school has a leaky roof that has not been fixed, organizing a group of well-spoken parents to address landlord, district, or even legislators can sometimes do the trick. It is difficult to believe that someone would by choice have a faulty facility where there are kids, but sometimes decision makers need a reminder that it's not just any building. It's a school.

Lack of a school kitchen can also present an issue for some families. Free lunches may not be a possibility for a school without a kitchen and this would affect students who rely on the federally subsidized lunch program. Depending on the charter school law in your state, receiving subsidized lunch at a charter may or may not be a problem. Again, remember that "no" is a bad word, and continuing to work with the school, authorizer, and government organizations responsible for the food program is key. Each of these groups is in place for the benefit of the children. A family should never have to choose between the right to food and the right to quality education. *If you find yourself in this predicament, flip to the back of this book for contact information to your state's education department, legislators, and/or charter school organizations.*

That was the bad news of charter school buildings. Now it's time to cover the perks. First of all, what does autonomy mean when it comes to school buildings? It means the freedom to seek different choices than the standard, cookie-cutter model designed for mass-produced education.

For example, Denver School of Science and Technology and has a facility of award-winning design. It was created as a "living laboratory" for the students in its school design, construction initiatives, and "green building" efforts. According to the school Web site the building design has "served as an exemplar in several ways," including teaching students about engineering, mathematics, green building, and construction. The facility boasts outdoor courtyards, flexible classrooms, and energy-efficient design, which supports a wireless laptop infrastructure. Visit www.scienceandtech.org for more information.

How about The Media and Technology Charter High School (known as MATCH) in Boston, MA? The school building is a renovated auto dealership and is missing both kitchen and cafeteria. However, the third floor of the school facility offers apartments for the school's tutors who receive stipends and free housing for their work. Visit www.matchschool.org for additional information.

Another charter school worked with a design group to turn an old laundry building into a state-of-the-art learning environment. The University Academy Charter High School is featured in many publications as this school and its architecture team took on this special project. This construction is a testament to what is possible when community, school, and families come together. For more information about this school, visit www.njcu.edu.

CHAPTER 17

Transportation

Charter Schools: The Ultimate Handbook for Parents has repeatedly hinted to what this chapter will read: you may need to arrange your own *ultimate* rides to your *ultimate* charter school.

Sure there *are* some charters that do have school bus services—but that is the exception, not the rule. At the risk of sounding like a broken record, the reason for lack of school-funded transportation is once again—funding.

I am not joking when I tell you there was one school year I was pleading with my husband to sell our home and move closer to the charter school. It was the year when I had a child in full-time school, one in part-time kindergarten, and the third in a part-time preschool with an opposite schedule. I was home for less than two hours per day and my car turned into a royal pit. The good news is that the frequent fast-food trips resulted in enough food under the seats of my car to have sustained a family of four for days at the time, should we have encountered a freak snow, or a flat tire that I didn't know how to fix. We ate, napped, and did homework in the family vehicle. I considered upgrading my car to a Griswold-style motor home to add onboard bathroom access, and having my mail forwarded to my purple Dodge Durango so I could just park overnight in the school parking lot. But just like the moving idea, these fantastic suggestions were vetoed by my husband. I am glad that the lack of oxygen from being in the car all day only affected one of us, and the other could serve as the source of wisdom, long-term planning, and revered sanity.

Instead of selling car and home for the sake of education, my brilliant husband added a word to my vocabulary—car pool! Carpooling with another family is a beautiful, wonderful experience, which those of us who were left to our own devices cherish. You simply find another family whose dwelling is nearby yours and you divide the schedule up to fit both your needs. You drive this shift, I'll do the next. You get the idea.

If you are really lucky you may find one of those very organized parents who enjoy setting other people's schedule. That's when you may receive a five-year calendar including holidays, teacher in-service days, and leap year, handed to you in form of a PowerPoint presentation and manual flashcards. With a parent like that in charge your car pool will be on autopilot.

Some wonderful charter schools even assist in coordinating car pool arrangements between the families. Many schools will even print the neighborhood name next to the family's information in the school phone book, so you can just scan the line and find your new best friends.

If all else fails and nobody from your school lives nearby, attempt to align your trips in the direction your child's school (work and errands). Not always possible, I know. But sometimes a boss is willing to budge thirty minutes on your schedule in exchange for your bringing work home, or a neighbor may have a child attending another school near yours, which may solve the dilemma for both of you.

Part 4
Choosing a Charter School

In Part 4:

18. Is a Charter School Right for Your Family?
    Questions you should ask yourself before charter school enrollment
19. Charter School Variety
    Traditional, open classroom, online—exploring charter differences
20. Research Guide
    Which school is the best fit for your family? School comparison worksheets
21. Charter School Enrollment
    Is there a charter school litmus test? Lottery, waiting lists, first-come-first-served, and other variances

To be or not to be a charter school family: that is the question.

As the beginning of this book declared, there is only one person who can decide which schooling option is best for your family and that is the parent.

OVERVIEW

- Part 4 is designed to help you make such a decision, regardless of the answer.

- What are some of the facts you should consider? What concessions may need to be made? Is this realistic for you? Which type of charter school may be a fit? How do you enroll in a charter?

CHAPTER 18

Is a charter school right for your family?

"Congratulations! It's a baby. On the way out of this delivery room, please read the fine print on the meaning of parenting and difficult decisions destined to surface within near the future. Check the boxes on breastfeeding vs. bottle, childcare or stay-at-home-parenting—and the one on making the right school choice for your wee lil' angel. From this day forth you alone are responsible for this person and that she or he has what she or he needs for a lifetime. Note that any mishandling of business stated in paragraph 1.0 through 999.9 becomes solely the liability of you—the parent. Also note the lack of return policy at the bottom. All claims of refund or exchange will be dismissed, even if based on a faulty product. I am sure this information was available at the time of conception. Thanks for your business. Please come again."—*Your Obstetrician, from the Imaginary Playbook of Parenting*

OK, so there isn't a playbook for parents, but there are times I wish for one. It would be nice to defer to such material in moments like this when I have to deliver some bad news: regardless of which self-help you use—this one included—there are no guarantees for an education happily after for your child…

…Welcome back. Did you just look at the jacket of this book to see how much you paid?

Here you are, more than half way through a book on public school choice, just to find that you may still muff up picking the right school for junior. I offer my condolences. It's a little fact many of us have learned the hard way. I, for example, committed a slew of research into schools for my oldest child, enrolled him in a reputable neighborhood school, only to regret it a few months later. Was it because the school and the teachers were terrible? No, my child's learning style was just not the right fit for that school.

So what is a parent to do then? Well, you return to the research. For good and bad, you now have more information about your child to use in your quest for your family's education eureka moment.

There really are just a few methods of choosing a school: Firstly, research your options to make an informed decision. Secondly, have your friends, family, or location of residence make the choice for you. Or thirdly, consult the advice of a higher power—such as the magic eight ball.

Without knocking option two or three, by reading this book it is assumed your preference is number one. What you are doing right now—researching school options—is in the opinion of many, the most effective method to increase the odds of actually finding the right school for your child, whether it's the first try or the seventh.

When it comes to deciding whether or not a public charter school in general is a good pick for your child, we can start with reviewing the chapters up until this point. Due to the range of charter school types, some of these topics may not apply to a specific school.

Rate these topics according from 1 to ten in level of importance to your family:

Topic:

    School bus
    Facility amenities
    Playground
    Cafeteria
    Library
    Art room
    PE hall
    Dress code/uniform
    Homework
    Extended days/school year
    Before/after-school program
    Increased work expectations
    Strict disciplinary codes
    Volunteer requirements
    District/state governing
    School autonomy
    Curricula differs from the district school
    Smaller class sizes
    Smaller school

This working list of what your family is seeking and what you may not be able to do without, is the stepping stone in deciding if a charter school is a feasible choice for you or not. Some charter schools are fully equipped and chock-full of what is listed above, so you don't know for sure if any of these items are missing until you call the school. If you have a list full of "deal breakers," you may want to save time by calling area charter schools and see if they offer the amenities to fit your taste buds.

For example, if you are dead set against school uniforms and your area charters have them, there is an issue. Although little Johnny will wear nothing but Spider-Man pajamas and purple Crocs, odds are the school will not make an exception in the dress code policy.

If, however, this list has helped you conclude that a charter school sounds like a great possibility for your family, we can now progress to chapter 19 and talk about what *kind* of charter you may find interesting.

CHAPTER 19

Charter School Variety

I stopped growing when I was thirteen years old. *Praise Jesus!* I was in the seventh grade and six feet, two inches tall.

My adult friend Ann is only five-feet tall on a good day. She's one of those pint-sized little pixies who have never had the pleasure of clocking her head in the doorjamb. Ann and I have very different needs. I have worn capri pants much longer than it's been fashionably acceptable. They are not capris per se. It's just how pants in general look on me. And when I fly in a commercial airplane, my knees are pulled up to my chin, and I always seem to find that one seat that does not lean back.

Ann, on the other hand, has a hard time seeing over the steering wheel when she drives her car. I offered her my daughter's booster chair for the driver's seat of the car. Apparently this presented another problem. Her feet were now dangling off the ground, and she could not reach the pedals. Ann and I drive very different vehicles. She's in an SUV with the seat pulled up close enough to lick the windshield and I drive a smaller car with my head sticking out of the sunroof. Both of us love our cars and would not consider a change…until 100,000 miles.

Imagine if there were only one type of automobile. It has wheels, a steering wheel, and gas and brake pedals. It goes from points A to B, just like any other variation would and will fit up to fifty of your "unseatbelted" best friends. It has a snazzy name too—semitruck.

Would you get one? Variety is good. The same comes to charter schools. The more venues of offering quality education we have, the more likely that there will be something for everyone. You will find that within a certain variety of charters there are multiple versions. So please use this chapter as a general guide, versus written in stone. However, this general description is a good guide in entertaining which charter choice may be a good pick for you.

Traditional classroom

Most people would define a traditional school setting as the classroom of several students and one instructor (perhaps with the added assistance of paraprofessionals). Learning consists of lessons, quizzes, homework, tests, and projects. The traditional class routine is considered structured, and subjects are scheduled with predictability. Some children thrive and learn well in this consistent environment.

Traditional charter schools are the ones most similar to district schools based on these criteria only. There are hundreds of varieties of traditional schools that not only separate traditional charters from district schools, but from each other.

Examples of traditional classroom charter schools:
    Alpha Academy Public Charter School, *Fayetteville, NC*
    Dolores Huerta Preparatory High School, *Pueblo, CO*
    Challenge Charter School, *Glendale, AZ*

Open Classroom

The open classroom concept originates from the one-room schoolhouses from long ago. The model was reborn in popularity in the United States in the 1970s. An open classroom may also be called a student-centered learning environment. Learning takes place based on the initiatives of the students, and not necessarily on the queue of the teacher.

Some styles of open classroom include children from multiple grades in one environment, and others offer multiple teachers and teach by student-to-student mentoring. There are also open classrooms that are taught outdoors, in courtyards, and in other settings in which the "learning facility" literally has no walls.

Examples of open classroom charter schools:
    Salt Lake City Open Classroom, *Salt Lake, UT*
    Ark Community Charter School, *Troy, NY*
    Audubon Charter School, *New Orleans, LA*

Online

The non-online school types (above) are considered brick-and-mortar-schools. This term describes the type of education that brings the student to a specific building. A true online charter school does not require a student to attend classes in a certain facility. Instead it is a cyber school that teaches courses primarily through virtual computer methods. This means that a student who learns better in a home environment can be schooled this way, but through a public charter school that is funded through taxpayer moneys.

Even though online charter schools have much in common with home-schooling, only 20% of online charter students are former students of homeschooling.

Examples of online charter schools:
   Blue Sky Online Charter School, *West St Paul, MN*
   Choice 200 Online Charter School, *Perris, CA*
   Colorado Virtual Academy, *Northglenn, CO*

Online/Brick-and-Mortar Hybrid

The blended approach to online schooling can provide an alternative for students who learn well using technology, but need the structure of going to a school building. Some hybrid online programs expect the student to attend a certain amount of hours per week at the facility, whereas others request daily attendance at the building while the learning is via computer.

A recent North American Council for Online Learning (iNACOL) report states: "Online learning is proving to be an important and sometimes transformational tool in reaching at-risk students. Most online programs serving credit recovery and at-risk students—but not all—have a significant face-to-face component. The blended approach is important because it provides expanded student support and face-to-face contact. The online component—whether fully online or blended—provides twenty-first century skills to a group of students who often have less than average exposure to computers and technology." *iNACOL's Promising Practices in Online Learning: Using Online Learning for At-risk Students and Credit Recovery*, written by John Watson and Butch Gemin.

Examples of Online/Brick and Mortar Hybrid charter schools:
    Trio Wolf Creek Distance Learning Charter School, *Lindstrom, MN*
    Eagles Peak Charter School, *Murrieta, CA*
    HOPE Online, *CO*

"Hope Online is among schools which are successfully implementing a hybrid model of online curriculum and face-to-face interaction. Each Hope Online student receives instruction via an individualized learning plan (ILP), an undisputed advantage of online education. By meeting students where they are and building upon that foundation, ILPs enhance student academic growth. Additionally, Hope Online's statewide network of community-based learning centers broadens student opportunities to engage in online curriculum and benefit from adult support and peer-to-peer collaboration."

—Hope Online

CHAPTER 20

Research Guide

There are a multitude of questions I did not ask before enrolling my son in a charter school. Not because I am dense, but because I had no idea what a charter school was and that one was different from another. It wasn't until after we were integrated into the fabric of the school that I began understanding the differences between the schools in my area. Thankfully it did not take long for us to find the charter school we were destined for. It was more luck than skill, that's for sure.

You, on the other hand, will have access to this handy-dandy handbook for charter school research. This charter school research guide is made possible with the help of the Independence Institute, The United States Department of Education Office of Innovation and Improvement, and a posse of charter school superparents. The back of this chapter features helpful links to these organizations.

The first evaluation will be geared toward the learning needs of *your child*. As mentioned in the beginning of this book, you may want to seek professional guidance for a more in depth consultation. Once you find what type of school you are seeking for your child it will become much clearer on whether or not a particular school is a proper fit.

The *school research worksheets* are geared toward differentiating between charter schools, but you could really apply this method toward any school. Make copies of these pages for your research so you can reuse this book, or add additional schools, which may not otherwise fit into the space allotted by the dimensions of this publication.

Step 1: Getting to know your student

When asking parents where to begin the search process for a school, there is a general consensus—start with evaluating the needs of the child!

By exploring what type of learner your child is and what he or she needs to be a successful student, you optimize the opportunity to find a suitable environment. How do you know which school is a good choice if you don't know what your child needs? What if none of the available options actually offer what your son or daughter requires? Would it matter if you have a dozen of the nation's top schools in your backyard if none of them offers the learning environment suitable for your child?

Research has long yielded that parental involvement is a key factor for student achievement. Learning more about your student is a good step in equipping you as a parent to be a part of his or her schooling experience.

The questions are designed to encourage discovery of who your child is as a student. Keep in mind that a student's needs may change over time. For example, a sixth grader may no longer need the one-on-one support he needed for reading in kindergarten.

Here are some questions to help you identify what type of learner your child is:

1. Your child needs an environment that is:
   structured
   less structured
   don't know
2. Your child learns better:
   by watching how things work
   by reading how things work
   by listening
   by participating in discussion
   by participating in projects or activities
3. Your child learns better while:
   working on his own
   working in a group
4. Your child needs:
   extra attention to finish a lesson or project
   challenging work
   language support (English is not a first language.)
   a learning specialist
5. My child has medical or learning needs not defined above.
   No
   Yes (List here.) _____

6. My child needs a program that is strong in:
   math
   reading
   writing
   science
   arts
   music
   Other: _____
7. What makes your child excited about learning?
   _____

8. My child is happier while socializing:
   One-on-one with another child
   Group setting
   Neither
   Either

Collect the information above and write out the description. It may look something like this:

"My child needs an environment that may or may not need to be structured. He learns by listening and while working in a group. My child needs additional support in learning English and more challenging work. My child does not have any medical or learning needs that require the attention of a counselor, doctor, nurse, or specialty aid. My child is very strong in math and art. He gets excited about learning when he is praised and senses his own accomplishments. He has a best friend, but also enjoys playing in a group of friends."

This list will be a trusty companion when you begin interviewing schools.

Step 2: Collect information about charter schools

Gathering information about schools is important, and it is recommended that you use several methods of attaining such knowledge. Include the following information sources:

- Visit the school. Call the school and set an appointment.

- Review the school report card to the community. This should be available on the school, district, or state Web sites.

- If possible, ask friends who have children at the school you are looking into.

- Attend school fairs and open houses.

- Ask the school to provide written material, such as brochures and welcome booklets.

- The Internet. Visit the school website, read the mission statement, the newsletters, and the parent handbook. Give your favorite search engine a whirl using the name of the prospective charter school. Keep caution that much on the Internet is dated, or based on opinion and cannot be classified as the gospel truth. But the Internet may tell you what others think about the school and what has made headlines.

- Contact your state charter school organization and the charter school authorizer (see chapter 25) and ask if there is additional information that you should consider prior to enrolling your child in that particular charter school.

What questions do you ask? Step three will give you a cheat sheet with questions frequently asked about charter schools. There is also room for you to add inquiries specific to your family.

Step 3: Use the charter school comparison guide

Here are helpful questions in comparing charter schools. Make one copy of this guide for each charter school you are researching. It may be useful as a side-by-side tool.

Academics

Does the school have a strong curriculum in the following subjects?

- Mathematics _____
- English   _____
- History   _____

- Science   _____
- Arts   _____
- Languages   _____
- Computer literacy/technology_____

What additional subjects does the school offer? _____
_____

Does the school have a special academic focus or theme? Describe.

_____

Does the school offer the following features?

- Advanced Placement   _____
- International Baccalaureate   _____
- High school honors courses   _____
- Gifted and Talented courses   _____
- Enrichment courses   _____

Is there an English language acquisition program? _____

Does the school staff someone fluent in the student's first language (if applicable)? _____

If your child has special learning needs, how would the school provide necessary support?

_____

Is the school open to look into additional services?
_____

What is the attitude of the staff regarding this topic?
_____

Which extracurricular activities are offered?
_____

What is the school rating according to the school report card?
_____

How do the school's state test results compare?
_____

If a child is falling behind, what would be considered a reasonable time frame for the parents to be informed and a plan put in place?
_____

How often do the children have physical education (PE)?
_____

What type of PE is offered?
_____

What sports are available?
_____

How often do students participate in?
- Arts
- Music
- Foreign Languages

How much time should be expected to spend on homework?
_____

Are there tutors or specialists available on campus?
_____

Are there study hall or study groups available?
_____

How is progress measured?
_____

Outside of test scores, what other methods are being used in evaluating progress? _____

Describe the school's character education program.

_____

Attitude

Is the staff friendly and welcoming? _____

Is the response to your phone calls and e-mails prompt and polite?

_____

How does the school communicate with its families? E-mails, newsletters, regular communication folders?

_____

What type of volunteer commitment is expected from the parents?

_____

What type of volunteer commitment/community service is required of the students?

_____

What types of volunteer opportunities are offered to the parents?

_____

What types of volunteer opportunities are offered to the students?

_____

Amenities

Is there organized school transportation? _____

Are there before-and after-school programs?

_____

Is there a school lunch program? _____

If needed, ask about arrangements for federally subsidized breakfast and lunch services. _____

Is there a gym? _____

Is there a cafeteria? _____

Is there an art room? _____

Is there a music room? _____

Is there a school library? _____

If not, what library services are in place?

_____

Are computers and technologies available to all students?

_____

Expectations

Is there a dress code? _____

Is there a school uniform? _____

What are consequences for dress code violations?

_____

What time does school start?

_____

What time does school end?

_____

What is the consequence for being tardy?

_____

What is the homework policy?

_____

What is the consequence for not turning in homework?

___

Is there summer school?

___

Is it mandatory?

___

How long is the school year?

___

How do I/my child contact the teacher with questions? Email, phone?

___

Learning environment

What is the school's approach to teaching? Project-based learning, traditional, student-centered learning, online, etc.?

___

How often are tests administered?

___

If it is an online school:

___

Are some lessons taught in real time?

___

Is there a requirement to attend facility-based lessons?

___

If so, how often and where?

___

Is technology provided by the school?

_____

What technology requirements need to be provided by the family?

_____

How large are the class sizes?

_____

Are the classrooms separated by grade, or mixed age groups?

_____

Is it a single sex school, or coed?

_____

Additional questions:

_____
_____
_____
_____

Step 4: Select a school

Use the information in (Step 1) "Getting to know your student" to cross-reference the school comparison guide. You may also wish to use the self-evaluation guide in chapter 18 "Is a Charter School Right for Your Family?" to make sure the "deal breakers" have been answered in the school comparison worksheet.

Congratulations! You have now completed thorough school research.

Next we will answer the most commonly asked questions regarding charter school enrollment.

Helpful resources in choosing schools:
    http://www.ed.gov/parents/schools/find/choose/choosing.pdf
    www.publiccharters.org
    www.yourcharterschool.com
    http://www.schoolchoiceforkids.org (Colorado)
    http://school.familyeducation.com

CHAPTER 21

Charter School Enrollment

"How did your kid get into that charter school?" If I had a nickel for every time I heard this question I could personally offset our national debt.

Much confusion and numerous rumors circling charter school enrollment policies. Do these schools cherry-pick the students? Of course not. They let my kids in.

In all seriousness, charter schools as public schools cannot choose whom to admit or not. Public charter schools are subject to all laws governing public schools, including civil rights and federal special education law. Due to the popularity of charter schools there is a common issue of more applicants than available capacity. As in most instances of school autonomy the process of what follows varies based on the particular school.

Let's take the mystery out of charter school enrollment.

1. The first step in applying for a charter school is to fill out an enrollment application. Contact the school of interest and request a form. You may apply online, by fax, or drop off in person. Ask the school which method is preferred.

> **Applications:** Just like any other public school, a charter school will ask the parent/guardian to complete an enrollment application. The purpose is to attain proper contact information and other relevant data. This is not an attempt to weed out kids whose mama dresses them funny. It is a very similar process you will find in schools across the nation regardless of being a charter. Some schools make applications available online. Most forms require information such as the student's name, address, phone number, birth date, current grade, name of last school attended, and school district. Some charters may ask if your child has special learning requirements, but most schools will wait for this question until after your child has been offered a

spot. Again, this question is not in place to size up a student's abilities, but information gathered to properly prepare for your child.

2. Ask the charter school of interest about its admission policies and important dates (open houses, potential open enrollment windows, lottery drawings).

Lottery admission: When the number of students outnumbers available student capacity, charter schools utilize one of two methods in completing enrollment. The most common procedure is lottery selection. These lotteries are usually open to the public and some charters even celebrate the occasion as an advertised special event. The names of the applicants are drawn randomly, often by the help of computer software designed for such purposes, and the lucky family has the opportunity to either accept or decline the enrollment. The benefit of the lottery process for those of us who dragged our feet in the school enrollment game is clear, as we are just as likely to get a spot for our children as those who turned in the paperwork during the postpartum period. Lottery selection is also the preferred method for families new to the area, as it offers the same chance of enrollment as someone who has lived in the district for generations.

First-come-first-served enrollment: This is what is called a "true waiting list." Charter schools that use this method of enrollment admit students based on the date that the application was completed. There are tales of desperate mothers making a stopover at the charter schools on the way home from the hospital to register their newborns for kindergarten. But don't fret if this was not you. Some of us (no names please) waited long and good before we started thinking about schooling for junior, but still got were able to enroll in our school of choice. Some charter schools have time stamps for the documents for assurance of fairness if there is more than one application per day. This is a prudent policy as images of the last turkey in the store the day before Thanksgiving, comes to mind.

If the school has a first-come-first-served enrollment procedure, request the number on the list your child is and the number of families usually contacted to fill the school year for that grade. For example, your child may be number 78 on the list for 48 kindergarten spots. This may sound dreary until you discover that the school typically calls a hundred families per school year to fill those forty-eight seats. Families move or simply change their minds. This may be to your good fortune!

Open Enrollment: Some, but not all charter schools, have an open enrollment period. After you find the school of your choice, pay close attention to any potential deadlines in the admission policy. An open enrollment may be offered at various times of the school year. Again, keep in mind that filing the paperwork does not automatically mean that your child has been offered a space. It is simply a step in the process. Usually charters with open enrollment subscribe to the philosophy of lottery enrollment. This would prevent situations similar to Christmas shopping when three popular video game consoles arrive for the fifty customers in line.

Sibling Policies: Most charter schools offer preferential enrollment for siblings of current students. Among charter parents we sometimes use the unofficial term "coattail enrollment." In other words, "The Smiths accepted a spot for their third grader and the lucky kindergarten sibling road in on his *coattail*." Siblings are given priority status for enrollment to permit families to keep intact at one school. If you have multiple children you would appreciate the complications that juggling numerous schools, schedules, and homework routines may present.

Employee policies: It is not uncommon for a charter school to extend "sibling-like enrollment privileges" to the children of a teacher or full-time staff member. The children of full-time staff are often given priority in enrollment to the school, which can be viewed as an employment perk. It is also a policy that may attract teachers to apply for work within a popular charter school.

State requirements: To find out specific details for your area schools, contact the charter school, district, or state education offices.

Fees: Charter schools are *free* public schools. There may be book fees and or similar expenses, just like in any public school. In some charter schools book and school supply fees may not exist, and in many cases exceptions are made for families who struggle financially.

3. And now you cross your fingers and wait for the call.

It is really that easy.

But heed these words of caution: if you move, or change your phone number or e-mail address, don't forget to update the information with the school of your dreams.

Wouldn't it be awful to find that you did indeed win the (admission) lottery, but nobody could call you to let you know? That's like losing your winning Powerball ticket, only worse. Your child's education is priceless.

But what if you changed your mind about the school? It happens. Maybe junior got accepted to a different school and you are really content. No worries. When the charter school contacts you tell them, "Thanks, but no thanks." It's been said before. Besides, the school likely has a thick list of hopefuls waiting their turn for that special call. If you are happy right now, but don't want to completely give up the chance of accepting enrollment another time, ask them to put you back in the lottery, or on the bottom of the waiting list. Who knows? You may really appreciate a call in a few years. If not, turn it down again. There is no limit to how often a family can enter a charter school enrollment application.

Another prudent policy is to submit applications to more than one school. If stars did not align and junior did not get into your dream school the first round, you may need a plan B. Who knows, you may love plan B so much that it eventually becomes plan A.

Part 5

The Charter School Life
Now That You Are a Charter School Family

In Part 5:

22. Volunteering
    How much, how often, and what do I do when I volunteer for my charter school?
23. Teamwork
    The teacher-parent-student relationship
24. Outreach and Networking
    Connecting beyond your charter school

Welcome to the family.

You already have good idea of what is expected from you as a parent. Now we will talk about your role as an ambassador of charter schools. Sure, you could just focus on the success of your own charter student, but many find themselves drawn into the broader school environment and beyond the four walls of your charter school.

> **OVERVIEW**
>
> Regardless of which role you decide to accept, part 5 will give you an idea of where to go from here.
> - How do you connect with other families? Where do you volunteer?
> - How do you build a relationship with your child's teacher?
> - How do you network with other charter schools?

CHAPTER 22

Volunteering

Definitions of volunteerism:

- Volunteerism is the willingness of people to work on behalf of others without being motivated by financial gain. —*en.wikipedia.org*

- The reliance on volunteers to perform an important social or educational function. —*en.wiktionary.org*

- Performing an act of kindness, freely giving of your talent, time, and effort for the simple fulfillment of community expectations. —*www.dearborncf.org*

Volunteerism is the most sacred charter school term. Most of these schools would not exist if it weren't thanks to a group of unpaid individuals generously investing their time and personal efforts into starting and driving the program. It is thanks to these folks that your child has a choice in public education. Now that you've decided to join the school and reap its benefits, you are about to become a contributing team member.

Charter schools are run on a shoestring budget and receive on average 20%[1] less in funding than traditional public schools. A portion of the budget shortfall is made up by families donating their time to make up for work which the school otherwise would have to pay for.

If fifty volunteers contributed twenty hours in one school year at the value of $10 per hour (the rate given by several charter schools as the value per hour), the school saves $10,000, which equals roughly half the salary of a kindergarten aid. Everywhere you turn and all things you touch in a charter school was made possible by a parent, teacher, student, or community volunteer. By donating your time to your school you will find an irreplaceable connection with other families. It is by involving yourself in your child's school that you will acquire a strong sense of patriotic pride associated with your education.

Most charter schools will ask each family to commit a set number of hours per school year in contributing to the school. The number of hours will vary, and so will the selection of volunteer opportunities. Some parents come skipping through the charter school doors elated to be included in contributing to the school, while others dread this part. But those who originally resist the call of volunteer duty often find a change of attitude when the appreciation and result of their work set in.

Here are some of the most common volunteer opportunities you may see on the request list:

• Classroom assistance: The job description of this duty may differ greatly. Perhaps you want to help in leading a reading group? Is math your passion? Consider being an extra set of hands during mathematics lessons. The art and music teacher may be hoping that you will share your skills and talents by teaching a special project or being a guest speaker. Are you an immigrant? The social studies teacher may ask that you speak about your experiences to the class while learning a specific cultural unit.

• Administrative work: The school may be short staffed during lunch periods or a change in personnel. Check of a few volunteer hours, run the copy machine, type newsletters, stuff weekly communications folders, file returned books back onto library shelves, or help order office supplies.

• Sign up for a special event: Is a book fair coming to your school? Is the drama club hosting a dinner theater? Did your school organize an open house to the public? Does the school science fair need extra judges? Who is organizing the classroom party? Are there enough drivers for a field trip? Can you bake a casserole for a teacher who is sick or make forty-eight cupcakes for teacher appreciation week?

• Join a parent school committee: Parent teacher organizations are always looking for an extra set of hands. So are the community outreach groups. If you have a knack for organizing hundreds of wrapping paper orders, baking pies, and social networking—you want to check these committees out. There are usually regular meetings that you can visit and find out what is happening in your school.

- Join the school leadership: The majority of charter schools seek parents who are interested in serving on governing boards. If you feel that you have a contributing talent in leadership, let your school know. Sometimes you have to be nominated for such a role, so don't lose heart if your name is not mentioned the first time. These meetings are open to the public and you, as a charter school parent, should attend these meetings to stay abreast of current issues. This will also prepare you to be a valuable voting board member when your call comes.

If you are a working parent with a thick schedule or have other limitations, the information above may have given you cold feet. Before you turn around and run for the hills, let me assure you that the schools have solutions for your common predicament. Talk to your school about your situation and ask for suggestions. The school may offer volunteer opportunities that you can do from home, such as cut out construction paper templates for a bulletin board, spring-cleaning Saturdays, or helping a teacher prepare for a special project. Don't forget that making an extra casserole or baking extra cookies to bring to a bake sale counts as volunteerism the same.

It is noteworthy that since charter schools are public schools they cannot ask you to leave the school for not meeting requested volunteer hours. Although the practice of parental involvement is a strong part of the culture in the majority of charters, it isn't so in all of them. There are charter schools that focus on at-risk youth where parents are asked not to volunteer. Often times it is because the home lives of some of the enrolled students are so volatile that the school wants to create a safezone for the children. Other nonvolunteering charters serve significant portions of low-income, socioeconomic groups and feel it would discourage parents from enrolling in their program.

However, if you *are* capable of contributing of your schedule, it cannot be stressed strongly enough how beneficial your involvement is to your child's school. A charter school's volunteer team is much like an army of ants—small, but mighty.

The reason why charter school parents have such a strong reputation is much thanks to the power that comes from a well-organized group of parents. Parental involvement in education is often defined as parents taking responsibility and participating in his or her child's academic process. Effective parental involvement in education should be defined as volunteerism that has benefits beyond personal gain.

Parents are expected to take responsibility and participate in their child's education. But your volunteerism becomes truly effective when the same hours you spend at your child's school also make improvements for other people's children.

If you are spending the hours volunteering anyway, why not make sure as many kids benefit from your donation as possible? Think of it as the best bargain you'll find and your time is the currency. For every hour of your time you can benefit one or hundreds of kids. Which is the better value? Aren't you glad to know that you are not the only one who values your time?

The children, whose folks may not be able to come to school for one reason or another, also benefit from your participation at school. Consider if you were the parent who could not volunteer at school due to an unfortunate circumstance. Imagine how meaningful it would be to have another grown-up spend that extra time in reading groups with your child, or teach him how to tie his shoe laces, or assist during a science project. If you then find yourself in a pickle in the future, there would be a posse of best friends you never knew you had coming to return the favor.

Lastly, this is the most *radical advice* of this chapter: do not wait for the school to ask you to volunteer. They might. But you know what is expected of you, so why make them ask twice? Besides, what kind of an example would that be setting for your child? If you postpone the responsibility you have accepted until the very last minute, can we expect different behavior from our kids? Perhaps that science project will get put off until the last minute because he is just too busy.

On that note, it is not just the parents who volunteer at charter schools, but students, too. Many charter schools require its students to volunteer. This practice is particularly common in middle and high schools. In some instances volunteerism is so heavily weighted it is a graduation requirement. Student volunteer projects may be called community service, because it is not limited to be completed on school grounds. Charter schools encourage the kids to become involved in community projects and volunteer organizations.

Volunteering make us compassionate individuals and good contributing citizens in our communities.

"Parents are a strong force for change on the educational landscape."

—*A Parent's Voice, www.parentalchoiceineducation.com*

[1] www.edexcellence.net/doc/Charter%2_0School%_20Funding%_202005%_20FINAL.pdf

CHAPTER 23

Teamwork

"Talent wins games, but teamwork and intelligence win championships."
—*Michael Jordan*

You've heard it before: there is no *I* in *team*.

But there is an *I* in *win*. And a winning school team is depending that *I* participate.

Each of us plays a different role in the education success. The student's responsibilities include classwork, homework, attendance, respectful conduct, active participation, and punctuality. A teacher's responsibility is to teach, while the parent's role is to support the teacher and student learning at home.

If any of us fail to do our part in achieving good education, results become much more difficult. Sure, a student could defy all odds by overcoming a shoddy teacher who has little interest in teaching and a deadbeat family situation. A teacher may also be able to drill some necessary facts into the head of an apathetic student without the help of a parent. The parent could force feed learning at home without the cooperation of the child and the teacher. But the process would be far more consuming of time and effort than the efficiency of having everyone aboard.

What makes a good team?

1. *Respect:* Honor and appreciate each other's differences and roles.

2. *Trust:* The team needs to feel confident in the other player's intentions, integrity, and dependability.

3. *Support:* The members stand by each other in favor of the well-being of the team. Most often this refers to the teacher and parent supporting one another's decisions for the benefit of the student.

4. *Communication:* The most crucial element in a team.

5. *Team Goals:* Student objectives are team objectives.

6. *Conflict Resolution:* A set plan in how to deal with disagreements will strengthen trust and create positive outcomes from unpleasant experiences.

7. *Utilizing team resources:* Each brings individual abilities and strength. Seek assistance from the other team members and recognize each other's specialization.

8. *Control Methods:* Accept responsibility for your own actions and always contribute your best participation.

How do you apply these principles and create a student-teacher-parent relationship?

1. Introduce yourself to your child's teacher.

2. Give the teacher your contact information and welcome him/her to use it.

3. Ask the teacher how you can best reach him/her.

4. Ask the teacher what his/her expectations are from your child.

5. Ask your teacher how you can best support student learning at home.

6. Go to conferences.

7. Attend open houses and back-to-school nights.

8. Read all written communications.

9. Write notes about questions, concerns, and compliments.

10. Address any existing unique needs your child may have and share known information in how to help him/her.

Communication is wonderful and necessary, but it needs to be done with finesse. The most well-intended parent-teacher interactions can sometimes result in an undesirable situation. Sure, it's your baby we're talking about and it's easy to become defensive when things are not one hundred percent sunshine, but our personal communication styles can have an impact on outcomes.

What are some best practices in conversing with your child's teacher and how do we prevent being perceived as a notoriously difficult parent?

- DO present a united front with the teacher in front of your child.

- DO treat the teacher as he/she is the most valuable asset of the school, second to your child.

- DO make yourself available.

- DO share your child's highlights and progress.

- DO tell the administration when a teacher goes above and beyond.

- Do extend your partnership and support both verbally and in writing.

- DO acknowledge the difficulty of the teacher's situation on sensitive topics.

- BE compassionate.

- DO let your child impress the teacher with his own skills.

- DO address concerns in a constructive manner.

- DO move on to other topics after solutions have been presented and agreed upon.

- DO openly forgive your child's teacher.

- DO apologize when you overstep your boundaries. Nobody is perfect.

- DO keep private conversations confidential.

- DO follow through on commitments.

- DO give the benefit of the doubt when tricky situations arise.

- DO be prompt in replying to communications or attending scheduled meetings.

- DO respect the teacher's time. Ask if it is a good time to talk, or if you should set up an appointment.

- DO listen to feedback and take it to heart.

- DO homework with your student.

- DO fulfill your volunteer commitment.

- DO ask for help by the school administrator should you sense a conflict.

- DO follow your school's grievance policy if conflict arises.

- DO "sleep on it" before reacting to controversy.

- DON'T overemphasize your child's super powers. You know he's the most special kid in the world. So does the teacher. She has a room full of the most incredible kids in the universe.

- DON'T put your child down.

- DON'T micromanage your teacher. Focus questions on the broader picture of learning, not the font type of the last newsletter. He/she is the hired professional.

- DON'T use your physical person in attempt to intimidate the teacher. A restraining order is not the best way to start off communications with the staff.

- DON'T whine.

- DON'T be needy. The teacher's attention should be on the kids, not the parent who needs constant assurance.

- DON'T overreact. The teacher said that Johnny did not do well on his last humanities test, not that he's the biggest failure in all humanity. There is a difference.

- DON'T form preconceived opinions on matters before addressing them.

- DON'T storm out on a teacher before he/she has had an opportunity to solve the issue.

- DON'T gossip. This is one of the most destructive behaviors that creates toxic results.

- DON'T call the evening news to report incidents that should be solved within the school. I am not kidding. There have been parents who have reacted to an event on campus by phoning the media instead of working with the school staff. This type of behavior is not only damaging to the persons directly involved, but can have a devastating effect for hundreds of students. Ask yourself what you are trying to achieve and if this is truly the best route.

- **UNLESS A LAW HAS BEEN BROKEN**: Give the charter administration a chance to address school issues before you call out of chain-of-command (e.g., authorizer). There are guaranteed to be a few layers of individuals between the teacher whom your complaint is with and the state education board (or applicable charter sponsor). Each charter school has a grievance policy. Please follow it step-by-step.

• DON'T write something in an e-mail you would not say in person.

Bringing learning components into your parenting is not just a wholesome practice, it's a wonderful bonding experience. Watching your child evolve as an independent reader, learn a new language, or do well on a report card brings amazing joy.

Many times we learn through our child's education, too. How long has it been since you read up on American art history, or geometric angles?

How do you build a strong parent-student relationship?

• DO homework with your child.

• DO review his/her report card.

• DO encourage and praise progress.

• DO present a united front with the teacher.

• DO support learning with trips to the libraries, museums, and other fun events.

• DO read with your child every night. If it is an older student, schedule a family reading time, or host a book club.

• DO answer your child's questions.

• DO call the teacher or another parent if you have questions on the homework.

• DO help your child prepare for projects.

- DO have a set time and place for homework.

- DO make schoolwork a priority.

- DO explain the value of an education.

- DO dream with your child about future professions and aspirations. Help your child see how his/her education will lead there.

- DO celebrate together.

- DO talk positively about the teacher and school.

- DO fulfill your volunteer commitment and teach your child the value about participating in community efforts.

- DO discipline when your child is not following the rules.

- DO attend school conferences, open houses, school plays, and other notable events.

- DO model desirable attitudes and behavior.

- DON'T do your child's homework for him.

- DO make school attendance and timeliness a priority.

- DON'T trash-talk teachers, staff, or other students.

- DON'T belittle school rules and expectations.

- DON'T justify your child's behavior in breaking school rules.

- DON'T accept tardiness, half-done work, and bad attitudes toward school staff and other students.

Help your child foster a student-teacher relationship:

- DO encourage your child to actively participate in class.

- DO encourage your child to raise his/her hand and ask questions.

- DO sign slips and notes brought home by your child.

- DO teach your child how to formulate a note or e-mail to the teacher when there are questions about homework.

- DO teach your child that the teacher is boss in his/her domain.

- DO teach your child that you do not accept disrespectful behavior towards staff.

- DO tell your child his teacher cares about him and his success.

- DO teach your child to properly address his teacher by title and last name.

- DO tell your child that his teacher is a person of trust.

- DO teach your child to be supportive of the teacher's wishes even when friends do otherwise.

- DO teach your child to accept responsibility for his/her actions.

- DO encourage your child to share his/her academic goals with the teacher.

- DO encourage your child in telling the teacher when he/she is finding a lesson particularly interesting.

- DO teach your child to apologize when needed and forgive when someone else makes a mistake.

- DO tell your child when his/ her teacher praises progress.

- DON'T tell your child to blame the teacher for poor student performance.

- DON'T defend a student's poor choices and decisions.

- DON'T accept work partially or inadequately completed.

- DON'T permit your child to speak disrespectfully about his teacher even when he/she is not around.

- DON'T tell a student the teacher is wrong or incapable.

"The way a team plays as a whole determines its success. You may have the greatest bunch of individual stars in the world, but if they don't play together, the club won't be worth a dime."—*Babe Ruth*

CHAPTER 24

Outreach and Networking

"As a parent, you have the right and responsibility to stand up and demand the best education for your child. It is important that you learn all that you can about how schools work, and then turn that knowledge into action for your kids."—*Parent Power! The Center for Education Reform*

Charter schools are dependent on its volunteers.

However, there is an additional group of volunteers not as often discussed, whose work a charter school cannot do without—*the charter school advocates*. The distinction between a charter *supporter* and *advocate* is very slight, but defining nevertheless. A *charter supporter* is someone who believes in charters, back the efforts, and often assists in school-specific functions. Most charter school volunteers would technically be classified as charter supporters.

A *charter school advocate* on the other hand, is a charter school supporter who is actively involved in the greater charter school community. These folks are the voices of charter schools that unite, organize, and communicate on behalf of the charter school movement.

There are plenty of times when charter schools and their families need to band together with other charters. Sometimes it's for the purpose of supporting each other's ventures or to bounce ideas off of one another. Other times it is for more serious business, such as a pending election, proposed legislation that will affect the schools, or rule changes from the charter authorizer that need collective decisions.

The strength of charter schools is in the joint passion from its members and supporters. Let's face it: the charter community is not the largest group in the education world. But when banded together, this collection of families, teachers, and community leaders is a force to be reckoned with.

Here is why. The average charter school in the United States serves three hundred students. The charter advocate is keenly aware that when standing up for joint issues, voices in numbers matter. Charter advocates are great information scavengers and keep records of area charters, families, and community leaders. When need be, whether it is a fun cause or serious matter that may have a negative impact on charters, the advocates know how to activate the grassroots network and equip folks with pertinent information.

Since you will find families and supporters of three hundred children at one charter school, imagine how quickly these numbers multiply when you enlist all the charters in a school district, state, or our nation. As of 2009, the United States of America has 1,385,325 students enrolled in 4,792 charter schools.[1]

If the charter school advocacy network activated the voice of every parent, teacher, grandmother, friend, and uncle to this number of students, you bet it is taken seriously.

These are not just any millions of individuals. The folks of charter schools are so enthusiastic about their education that some critics have held the belief that someone went and solicited these families. Truth is that delight for success is contagious and easy to be excited about.

The power of one individual's passion for education is significant and can have tremendous impact for the benefit of millions of children. Look at people like professor Ray Budde, who began the charter school movement, or Mike Feinberg and Dave Levin, two young teachers who founded KIPP, an incredible network of charter schools that gives millions of inner-city children a quality education, or Charles Reich, the English teacher of professional football Hall of Famer, Steve Young, who had drilled into him, "You are smarter than you think you are."

Fact is that you don't need to be a teacher, a legendary professor, or even a professional athlete to make a difference. The most important person who can make a difference for your child's education is you!

Advocacy does not have to take a lot of time. There are several effective methods in which you can make a significant contribution to our charter schools. An advocate is also not a cover word for extremist. So please, no visions of lying down in front of school buses, or opening the doors to underperforming schools to set knowledge-impoverished students free.

Charter advocates are regular people who serve as the voices for such schools. Here are several easy steps ways in which you can go from a *charter school supporter* to a *charter advocate*:

Charter school organizations:

There are wonderful support organizations throughout our nation whose purpose is to serve as a resource to the charter school community. These groups are committed to helping charter schools in reaching higher levels of success by providing information, resources, technical support, *advocacy*, public relations assistance, and strengthening charter school laws, contract negotiations, charter application reviews, start-up support, and more.

There are varying types of charter organizations, some that are state-based and others that serve the national audience. Few of our grassroots efforts would be possible without these organizations as they provide an invaluable element for our families. Charter school organizations are to charters what Google is to the Internet. It is the go-to source on information, news, and events.

Many charter school organizations provide an advocacy network as part of their services to involve active charter families in events and activities.

Contact your charter school organization today and find out how you can participate.

US Charter Schools: www.uscharterschools.org

National Alliance for Public Charter Schools: www.publiccharters.org

The Center for Education Reform www.edreform.com

Each of these links above provides information about charter school organizations by state.

Board Meetings

Supporting your charter school in your community may only be a board meeting away. You should attend meetings for your school's governing board as well as the ones offered by the authorizer's board of education. It is important that you understand current issues surrounding the charter, which may have direct impact on the school. A fundamental key to a healthy relationship between charter board and that of its authorizer is also to have a solid understanding of each other's functions and purpose.

Build relationships

Do you have the gift of gab? How about the talent of diplomacy? Consider being involved in relationship building with your school district, authorizer, community members, businesses, other charter leaders, and politicians. The name of the game is often to be open minded, to think outside the proverbial box, and to use artful compromise.

Imagine how handy it is to know someone when you need to ask for his or her support in return. If your school is going through building construction, charter renewal, audits, proposals for expansion, requests for inclusions in financing, or petitions for law changes, you will soon find how valuable preexisting network connections are.

Is there an election coming up? Who is running? Is that person supportive of charters? Make sure you know your candidates. Talk to them. They are not as intimidating as they may appear. Is one of the candidates unfriendly to charters? Why? Can you or someone in your charter organization settle the concerns? If the candidate remains unfriendly to your children's school, be thankful that you are now an informed voter who can support someone else. Remember elected officials are elected by you and work for you! Work with your charter school organization and create lists of charter school friends and foes for elections. Consider volunteering for charter-supporting campaigns.

Get political

Read up on proposed laws and stay abreast in the media about upcoming policy changes. More on this in part 7.

Write policy makers

Local and national charter organizations send action alerts for pertinent proposals. When needing your support, the group will e-mail you the reason and a template for you to complete. It is very simple. The charter organizations will automatically forward your e-mails to the applicable addressees.

Write the editor

Many newspapers are excited to print the views of its readers. Participate in civic dialogues or weigh in on urgent issues to show your support.

Blog

A blog is a type of Web site maintained by an individual with regular entries of commentaries, events, and opinions on current issues. It is a rapidly growing form of entertainment and sometimes even viewed as a news source. Anyone can start a blog and most of the time it's free. Many newspapers and media sources offer free blogs for readers to add materials to the site.

Blog about your charter school experience and share the topic du jour.

In the online world even the mundane can be humorous, or at least relatable to readers. Did your kid forget his lunchbox again? What's worse: that your school does not offer a lunch program, not even a crappy one, or that the tuna on rye that got left under the backseat really smells like tuna and rye by noon?

Have fun with it. Blog topics are for starting conversation and generating interest. What could possibly be more interesting than your life in a charter school?

But heed the warning from experience and don't write something you wouldn't say in person.

Join a grassroots network

Find like-minded individuals like yourself in local charter groups. Often your charter school organization can help you locate these groups, or start your own. Create an environment for charter families to information share and join in mutual, local charter projects. Together you can network, blog, write the editor, and build relationships with community leaders.

Ask

Inquire with your school director, board, and your favorite charter school politicians what more you can do. Perhaps there is a special project coming up that you can assist in.

Vote

VOTE! VOTE! VOTE…

…Did I say vote? This is one of the most powerful weapons you have in defense of charter schools. Don't just vote yourself, but inform others about ballot issues and school choice friendly candidates. If you don't vote, how can you later complain when the better candidate didn't win?

Besides, isn't relationship building and networking much easier when it's with someone you actually voted for?

Join a parent union

You read it right. It isn't just teachers who have collective bargaining power anymore. Parents do, too! The Los Angeles Parents Union is an alliance of organizations and families who are fed up with sending their kids to notoriously bad schools. The Web site says, "For too long, everyone else has been in charge of our children's schools. Politicians, bureaucrats, and special interests—they had the power. We were told to do the bake sales. Now it's our turn to take back the power over children's education. We are the only ones who will always stand up for our children—no matter what."

If you don't have a parent union near you, start one. Visit www.parentrevolution.org for more information.

Example of a parent advocacy effort:

"Amazing Press Conference and Rally!"

This morning saw the official kick-off of the Parent Revolution, and it definitely started with a bang. Over 200 parents turned out to Gertz-Ressler High School, one of the highest performing charter schools in Los Angeles, to declare that the days of parents sending their children to failing schools are over. There was an incredible lineup of speakers; parents desperate to improve their own schools, community leaders like Fernando Espuelas, and even politicians who agreed it is time to hand over power to the parents.

Gertz-Ressler High was the perfect place to launch our revolution, for one simple reason. Gertz-Ressler is taking the same exact students whom LAUSD is failing 97% are black or Latino, 95% qualify for free and reduced lunch and sending 97% of them to college. That's right: 97%. And the most incredible part is that they aren't doing anything magic[ical], just simple, common sense that others could easily replicate. They hold their teachers and administrators accountable. They have a small school with only 500 students, so students are held accountable as well. They stress real parental involvement, not just bake sales or magazine drives. Like Fernando Espuelas said today, "We know how to build great schools." It's inexcusable that we don't have more of them. And this is precisely what the Parent Revolution will change."—*Gabe Rose, Parent Revolution (CA)*

Get involved. Please visit the following Web sites:

www.publiccharters.org
www.parentrevolution.org

---

[1]This estimate is provided by the National Alliance of Charter Schools. Firm numbers for 2008-09 were not yet available from IL, MD, MI, NH, NJ, NY, SC, and WY, so 2007-08 data was used for these eight states.

Part 6

Behind the Scenes

In Part 6:

25. The Creation
    Who can start a charter school? What is a charter school authorizer? Management Organizations and Entrepreneurial Schools
26. Funding
    Show me the money. Who pays for charter school education?
27. Accountability
    To whom do charter schools answer and why? What is a SAC?

If charter schools were a Hollywood feature, this section would be the screen credits.

It is the honorable mention which informs you who this educational experience was made possible by.

As school choice connoisseurs we appreciate the fine product of a good charter school education, but how did this come about. Who started your charter school? How is it funded? Is it kept accountable? Can a school be autonomous and accountable at the same time?

Well, push those 3D glasses up on your face, keep the popcorn buttered and get comfortable.

OVERVIEW

Part 6 will cover the behind the scenes of the full length charter school feature.

CHAPTER 25

The Creation

In the beginning was *the word.*—John 1:1 (NIV). In the case of your charter school it was more likely a *thought*. Someone or a group of someones decided that your community needed an alternative program to what was already being offered.

Charter school founders can be parents, community leaders, businesses, teachers, school districts, educational entrepreneurs, and municipalities. Each of these entities brings a different facet to a charter school project, each important to the aspect of creating and operating the program.

Parents who create charters are often motivated by the very needs of their children that may not be met in existing schools. The passion and drive behind these individuals are hard to match. As pointed out by several of the starting groups, parents of this sort crop up at all stages of the chartering process and may or may not be the actual first people on the scene.

Imagine having a child in a sticky schooling situation, then come to find out that a group of professionals are starting an alternative program that offers a potential solution. In response many parents join the charter founders with active interest in pursuit of a successful school start-up.

Lisa Nolan, parent and founder of North Star Academy (CO) and former employee of Edison Learning, pointed out that a variety of skill sets are required to successfully execute a charter school start-up project. She wisely adds, "A person or groups wanting to start a charter school should not shy away because they don't possess all the know-how of a project. Yes, you need educators, an administrator, and business knowledge, and so on. *If your group does not have some of this you recruit it!*"

A charter school's start-up process is time-consuming and requires thoughtful research. The quality of such research will indicate to the school's potential authorizer whether or not this is a project to be taken seriously.

The charter school founders need to survey the scene, assemble a team, investigate laws, review chartering agencies' policies, assemble a core founding group, design a school plan, and plan, draft, and present the charter application. These are all steps that need to be completed prior to the mere approval of the school's existence by the charter authorizer.

This is one of the reasons why founders may contact a management organization for charter start-up assistance. Although involving a management organization is not a required step in the process, these businesses bring expertise within the field. Some management companies offer à la carte management services, meaning that a founding group may be able to purchase certain services without committing to the entire package.

Charter Management Organizations (CMO) may actually be founders on their own and apply for a charter from the authorizer (*see part 2, chapter 4 "The Leadership"*).

Education Management Organizations (EMO) can usually not hold the charter, but be instrumental in how it as attained for the founding group (*see part 2, chapter 4 "The Leadership"*).

Entrepreneurial charter schools, such as KIPP, use a franchise-like model. KIPP founders find training, business format, branding, and support through the organization. Unlike other types of franchises (e.g., fast food) KIPP promotes significant amounts of freedom for each school to develop its own flavor of local KIPP success.

In many ways, charter organizations power-tool shop for individuals who wish to run a school of its type. Each business offers services and equipment to empower and support innovation and promote education excellence.

Again, what the management organizations provide is something that is offered to charter founders, but it's not a prerequisite. There are plenty of wonderful charter schools that have been started from scratch by a few inspired individuals.

Charter School Authorizers

"[Charter school authorizers] are the entities that decide who is worthy of a public funds shepherd, and—more importantly—who is worthy of the responsibility for the lives of children every day."—*Susie Miller Barker, Vice President for Research & Evaluation, National Association of Charter School Authorizers (NACSA)*

Who can *authorize* a charter school? It depends on your state. Nearly 90% of public charter school authorizers are local school boards. They authorize about half of all charter schools. State boards of education and higher education (universities) authorize the most schools per agency. Certain jurisdictions—for example, Arizona and Washington, DC—have established public boards for charter school authorization. Some municipalities, such as the Milwaukee City Council, have the power to authorize charter schools. The mayor of Indianapolis has direct authority to approve charters. There are also a few cities that have mayoral control of education, for example, Chicago and New York.

The founding members file the charter application with the authorizer (sometimes called sponsor) who in turn decides whether or not the school is to be approved. But the authorizer's work does not end there. The charters are held accountable by its authorizer to deliver a desirable educational outcome as well as fiscal responsibility (*see chapter 27 "Accountability"*).

It is exceedingly important that a charter school maintains a healthy relationship with its authorizer. The sponsor is the quality control organization that assures the public that the taxpayer funds are being well stewarded by the charter and resulting in desirable education for our kids. Charter schools, on the other hand, are the businesses that will need to show good return on investment for the taxpayer by reporting to the authorizer.

It is when teamwork between these two groups is strong that innovation and education quality is at its best. As with any other relationship, good communication is key.

Since parents often serve in charter school leadership roles, it is important for us to have a broad view of our authorizers. Here are a few facts charter school authorizers around the country would like you to know:

What is a charter school authorizer?

SUNY Charter Schools Institute (New York): While the specific responsibilities of an authorizer may vary by statute from state-to-state, generally authorizers are the organizations to which individuals can apply to open a new charter school. Authorizers are generally charged with the ongoing oversight and evaluation of approved schools, reporting to the public on each school's progress, and considering each school's requests for charter revisions and applications for charter renewal throughout their existence.

What makes a good authorizer?

POLK County School Board (Florida): A charter school authorizer needs to have the capacity to provide the services charter schools need, the expertise to provide those services, and a desire to support charter schools and the students served in those charter schools.

What is the benefit of being the type of authorizer you are (higher education, municipality, district, state, etc.)?

POLK County School Board (Florida): The biggest advantage in being a district school authorizer is that the capacity and expertise needed to support the charter schools are already in-house at the district. In addition, our district can provide charter schools with additional services at no charge, such as including them in the training for teachers, paraprofessionals, and administrative staff or district grant proposals. The district can also provide services at the actual cost of these services to the charter school such as transportation or school lunches.

Districts also have a built-in incentive to assure that charter schools and the students they serve are successful, since these students will return to the school district once they have reached the highest grade level at the charter school. In the case of charter high schools, most of these students were district students, and are counted toward graduation rates, test results, school grades, etc.

The Indianapolis Charter Schools Initiative in the Office of the Mayor: The Mayor of Indianapolis is the only mayor in the country with the direct authority to charter new public schools. This unique authority—the city's CEO also being a charter school authorizer—enables the mayor to support the charter system in multiple ways. As a charter champion, the mayor has an array of political, financial, and governmental resources at his disposal that make for valuable allies for a growing and thriving charter sector. The mayor's intimate knowledge of the local community also makes the mayor-as-authorizer model valuable. Finally, there is a singular point of accountability in this model making public access, transparency, and accountability vital elements of this system.

What is the difference between your type of charter school authorizing agency and others in your state?

SUNY Charter Schools Institute (New York): SUNY is the largest authorizer in New York State, with forty-nine charter schools currently in operation located all across New York State. The New York State Board of Regents, which oversees New York's State Education Department, is also a statewide authorizer. The Board of Regents has twenty-four charter schools in operation. In addition, local school districts in New York can also serve as authorizers. To date, only two have done so: the New York City Schools Chancellor who has approved forty schools to date, and the Buffalo City School District which has approved two schools to date. SUNY's commitment to respecting a school's independence and autonomy is probably the most distinguishing characteristic about our work. We see the charter as a flexible document that may need to be modified over time as schools take in students and work to meet new challenges. Importantly, that respect is balanced by rigorous accountability requirements and the willingness to close those schools that do not fulfill their promises to parents.

The Indianapolis Charter Schools Initiative in the Office of the Mayor: The Mayoral Office of Indianapolis: Under Indiana law, local school districts, public universities, and the Mayor of Indianapolis have the authority to authorize charter schools. Aside from the mayor, the only other active authorizing agency in the state is a public university.

NYC Charter Schools: The NYC Department of Education is a risk-taking authorizer. We are willing, as an office, to take a chance on a charter applicant that has a novel or unconventional idea for a charter school.

When, why and how should a founding charter school group consider selecting your organization as its authorizer (given a choice)?

NYC Charter Schools: If the group seeking a charter doesn't yet have a track record but has a sound idea for a school, our office is the place to go.

The Indianapolis Charter Schools Initiative in the Office of the Mayor: The mayor's office designed a comprehensive application review and monitoring process that holds applicants to high standards. In so doing, we have drawn from the experiences of successful charter school sponsors and the research of experts from across the country. Through this process, we closely scrutinize charter school proposals to ensure that only proposals that include well thought-out plans, high standards and goals, and high levels of accessibility are chartered. The selection criterion also leaves the door open for applicants proposing to try approaches that are innovative and highly likely to work with their target populations. To advise the mayor on the selection of the most qualified applicants, he appointed the Mayor's Charter School Advisory Board, consisting of experienced local educators and community leaders. Application rounds are built around applicants' readiness. Applicants are encouraged to contact the Mayor's Office to discuss proposed plans.

The Mayor's Office has extremely high standards for entry. Only about 22% of people who have applied for a charter through the Mayor's Office have received one. These data are not meant to deter any operators from applying, but one reason for the success of schools authorized by the mayor is the high standards for entry.

SUNY Charter Schools Institute (New York): SUNY currently has two formal calls each year for new school applications, a winter and summer cycle. Applicants have told us they appreciate our high focus on standards and our respect for school's independence and autonomy. SUNY has a comprehensive new school application kit that is available on the Web site of the Charter Schools Institute at: http://www.newyorkcharters.org or by calling 518-433-8277, ext. 2051.

What does a parent need to know about their schools' authorizer?

NYC Charter Schools: That the authorizer isn't the "boss" of a charter school in the way that a district is over a regular public school. The board of a charter school is the authority over what happens at that school.

SUNY Charter Schools Institute (New York):

It is important for charter school parents to understand the standards to which their child's school is being held. In many cases, the school's authorizer can be a good source of information. SUNY's Web site includes a section for parents and also details all expectations for the schools it authorizes: http://www.newyorkcharters.org. Proactive parents can ask the school to share with them how the school is doing in relationship to those standards. And where there are deficiencies, parents can question what the school is doing to correct those deficiencies. Related to this is an understanding of the renewal process the school will undergo; not only how it works, but also the anticipated time frame.

POLK County School Board (Florida): The school should first realize that a charter school is an independent public school, therefore it has a great deal of local autonomy for decision-making purposes. The role of the charter school authorizer is to support the school and the students and parents of the charter school as outlined in the charter school's contract and application. In Polk County, each school's contract, amendments, contact information, and other relevant information is posted on the school board's Web site.

In Polk County, we have a choice specialist who is specifically designated to work with parents both in selecting the appropriate school, and to work with the school and parents to mediate any issues that arise. The process for our parent mediator is first to direct parents to work with the school staff, then the school's governing board, and then with staff from our office. Our parent mediator will assist parents in contacting the appropriate staff and setting up appointments, accessing information on our Web site and via public information requests, as well as contacting governing board members.

The Indianapolis Charter Schools Initiative in the Office of the Mayor: The mayor is typically the most visible public figure in a given community, and parents understand they can contact the mayor's charter school office in the event of problems that are not being effectively resolved at the local school level. In addition, parents should know that existing public charter schools authorized by the mayor have gone through a rigorous application process and are held accountable for high results after opening. Parents should know that the mayor takes the education of students seriously and has very high expectations for school performance.

If serving on a charter school board, what should the reader know about interacting with you?

SUNY Charter Schools Institute (New York): As board members, parents will want to carefully review the schools' charter and the board bylaws. Both documents, while cumbersome, are vitally important to understanding the scope of the responsibilities of a board member. Each document contains information about what is expected of the school and its board, and the extent to which the school board interacts with its authorizer.

POLK County School Board (Florida): When serving on a charter school's governing board in Florida, the first thing the governing board member should know is that they must participate in governing board training within the first six months of becoming a governing board member. This Department of Education training will provide an overview of their roles and responsibilities, the requirements of the public records law and the Sunshine Law, as well as other relevant statutes and governing board requirements.

Secondly, our office is always available to answer questions and assist a governing board member. There are a number of resources available both online and via our office. It is always helpful to have a governing board member who is familiar with the contract and with the Florida charter statute.

What should a parent avoid when interacting with the school authorizer?

POLK County School Board (Florida): A parent should appropriately and reasonably choose when to involve the charter school authorizer. The first thing a parent can do is to state the issue calmly and succinctly. A parent may be frustrated or have repeated the situation to a number of others; however, the authorizer's staff is most likely addressing this issue for the first time. Secondly, the parent should have information on previous attempts to address these issues at the school level. If not, the authorizer will suggest that this problem be handled at the school level first. An obvious exception to this would be an issue that involves the health and safety of students and/or staff.

A parent should also understand the role of the school and its governing board, which is to oversee and determine day-to-day operations of the school and the role of the sponsor, which is to assure broad implementation of the charter school as defined by the contract between the school and sponsor. For example, it is the sponsor's role to assure that each charter school student is afforded the opportunity for a nutritious, well-balanced lunch. It is not the sponsor's role to assure that Mary no longer has to sit next to Susie at the lunch table.

What are some of the questions a parent should ask when seeking a charter school?

SUNY Charter Schools Institute (New York): What are the school's goals? Is the school meeting its goals? What does the school expect from every student? What does the school expect from parents? Is the school doing better academically than the district school my child would attend? What percent of students are proficient in math and in English language arts? How long has the school been open? When does the school next apply to have its charter renewed? Do you think the school's charter will be renewed and if so why? How do parents know if the school is doing well? How will the charter school help my child to succeed? What role do parents play at the school? How long is the school day? How long is the school year? How many students are in each class? Does the school have a parent organization and if not, how is parent input sought? Does the school have a management partner and how do I find out more about them? Who is the school's authorizer and how do I find out more about them?

What specifics does an authorizer look for to grant a charter?

SUNY Charter Schools Institute (New York): There are countless factors that go into a high- quality application. Some of the most essential would be:

- Has the planning team done its homework? Have they visited other charter schools? Have they met with charter school leaders and board chairs? Have they reviewed applications that have been recently approved by the authorizer they are applying to?

- Does the application include a clearly defined curriculum aligned with state standards?

- Has the applicant team demonstrated that it has dedicated sufficient resources to professional development, remediation, serving students who need special education services, serving students who are English language learners?

- Does the application include a fully developed assessment system, including what assessments will be used when, and how assessment results will be communicated to teachers and used to improve instruction?

- Do the proposed school board members represent a broad range of skill areas: education, finance, legal, real estate, and individuals with previous nonprofit board experience?

- Has the leadership structure of the proposed school been clearly defined with each position having a clear set of responsibilities?

- Does the application present a school that will be organizationally, fiscally, and legally sound?

What specifics does an authorizer look for to renew a charter?

POLK County School Board (Florida): In Florida, there are consistent key elements when renewing a charter, but each district has the latitude to develop their own renewal process. The key elements found in the renewal process are the same key questions that are a part of the application and monitoring processes. These include:

- Is the academic program a success?

- Is the school a viable organization?

- Is the school's program and operation faithful to the terms of its charter?

What specifics does an authorizer look for when closing a charter?

New York City Charter Schools Office: Charter school closures, although painful, may be necessary to avoid the kind of persistent failure that often plagues terrible district public schools. Better that a charter school should close, then it should continue to operate year after year, under-serving the students who attend.

The Indianapolis Charter Schools Initiative in the Office of the Mayor: Lack of success in any area of the performance framework is cause for concern. Sustained lack of success in any area without a plan to quickly and effectively remedy deficiencies will result in swift action, including charter closure or nonrenewal.

SUNY Charter Schools Institute (New York): For SUNY, the driving factor in a school closure is failure to meet or come close to meeting the goals outlined in the school's academic accountability plan or the specific conditions of the charter agreement. SUNY makes every effort to focus the decision on what is in the best interest of the students. We know that all parents want their child in a small, safe environment where teachers know them by name. However, if the majority of the students in a school cannot read, then the school has failed those children, their families, and the broader community.

POLK County School Board (Florida): There are two types of charter school closures in Florida. The first is an immediate termination, in which a school is closed immediately if a sponsor determines that there is good cause, such as gross financial mismanagement, illegal activities, or the health, safety, or welfare of students is threatened. In such cases, the school district in which the charter school is located will assume operation of the school until issues are resolved and in most cases, until the end of the school year.

The second is a ninety-day termination process that is also outlined in Florida Statutes 1002.33. This happens when a school is not making appropriate academic progress, there are ongoing financial problems at the school, or the organizational structure of the school is not functioning appropriately. The symptoms of these problems can surface in a number of ways: a school that is operating in the negative for an extended period without a working financial recovery plan, a school where students are not making academic progress as outlined in their charter agreement, governing boards that are not meeting or violating the Sunshine requirements, etc. Usually a sponsor will attempt a number of interventions prior to recommending closure, and there is a process whereby the governing board of the school can appeal a sponsor's decision to close a charter school.

Read more from some of the charter school authorizers on school closings in chapter 32

For more information, please visit the following Web sites:
    http://www.uscharterschools.org/pub/uscs_docs/r/steps.htm
    http://www.qualitycharters.org/i4a/pages/index.cfm?pageid=1
    www.publiccharters.org
    NYC Charter Schools: www.nycchartercenter.org
    State University of New York Charter Schools Institute:
        www.newyorkcharters.org
    Polk County Public Schools: www.polk-fl.net/
    Indianapolis www.indy.gov/eGov/Mayor/Education/Charter

CHAPTER 26

Funding

Charter schools are public schools that are funded according to enrollment. The schools receive state and federal funding on a per pupil revenue (PPR) basis. Charter schools require full funding and fiscal autonomy to operate efficiently.

As independently run schools, the charter leadership must have decision power over finances. While being public schools, charter schools should be entitled to the same amount of government funding as conventional public schools. Many states and districts charge charter schools fees and "administrative costs," where more progressive state laws provide full funding for charter schools. The exact portion of the PPR that is allotted to the charter school is determined by the state legislature, or in some cases negotiated in the charter contract.

At a national average charter schools are funded at $6,585 per pupil, whereas a conventional district school receives $10,771 per student. This equals to charter schools receiving 39% less funding than the traditional schools.[1] For a school with five hundred students, that is a two million dollar funding gap per year. Collecting the money is left to the charter and not always as easy as it sounds.

"Soon after Vaughn Next Century Learning Center Charter School (San Fernando, CA) opened, Yvonne Chan charged that the district had shortchanged the school $811 per pupil. State funding called for $3,111 per pupil, but the district delivered $2,300. LAUSD responded that elementary schools receive less than junior and high schools. Moreover, a legal settlement that equalized funding for suburban and urban schools hampered further funding. Chan felt that violated the intention of the charter contract. She sent back the check and prepared to operate the school with a second mortgage on her house. In the midst of the controversy, Assemblyman Richard Katz drafted a bill requiring the district to give Vaughn 95% of the money it received from the state for its pupils and the school board backed down and paid Vaughn an additional $500 per student. The law set a precedent for charters' per pupil fund allocation. Says Chan, "We got that money because we went to war."—*Just the FAQs, CER 2009*

Another difference in funding is that traditional schools receive funding to cover the cost of securing a facility. Charter schools do not. There are a few exceptions to the rule, primarily when an existing conventional school coverts to a charter. In those cases the building already exists. Some states offer start-up capital funding for charter schools and a few school districts offer unused space for their charter school teammates. But in general, charter schools finance school building costs through independent means like fundraising, grant writing, donations—and often—by dipping into the per pupil revenue.

Another public school funding type is categorical federal education grant funds. These moneys are either distributed directly through an application process by the U.S. Department of Education, or dispersed by state agencies by various methods. State agencies tend to make decisions on such funds and charter schools based on whether or not a charter is recognized as its own local education authority.

This clearly begs the question, how do charter schools manage on such little moneys? Creativity, my friend, creativity! With the freedom of fewer regulations, charters explore various venues of doing things differently and cheaper. That does not mean it is not a struggle. The most common reason for charter school closures is insufficient funding.

Charter schools are incredibly inventive when it comes to school buildings. Retail strips, churches, warehouses, lofts, old businesses—all can be rented or purchased for the purpose of education. Many charter schools hold out to purchase school buildings until the school is established enough to get reasonable loan rates.

The charter schools' best friend in capital construction and start-up cost is sweat equity. School founders manage with the help of philanthropically motivated financial assistance of private funds, alternative credit routes, and many, many man-hours donated by willing volunteers.

There have been many classrooms painted by parents with the donated mismatched paints from the hardware store, classrooms furnished with the discarded desks from better-off schools, and school library shelves filled with tattered, donated books from across town.

It isn't just in facility funding where charters are innovative. Since charters set their own budgets, there is a freedom in how to spend such funds. Although often lacking the bulk purchasing power of a school district, charter schools can use alternative channels for services and supplies.

Having the freedom to choose your vendor and select services can at times be more cost-effective than purchasing in volume. Think of it this way; if you are in the market for a pair of sneakers, purchasing a bundle of them at a discount warehouse will not save you money if it is not what you need. You need a pair of size 9 athletic shoes, but the prepackaged bundle is a dozen of size 5 sneakers—left foot only.

The inference is not that all district purchases are of poor quality, but that volume purchasing does not necessarily equal cost savings.

Author's note: Charter critics often comment that the extra money is needed for the district schools, as it is a larger operation. It is interesting that it is usually the same critics that say charter school education is costlier than the one of a conventional public school student. I have looked at the numbers over and over again, but I still can't get 39% less funding to equal more than 100%.

---

[1] *Based on information from 2008 Annual Survey of America's Charter Schools by the Center for Education Reform:* www.edreform.com/index.cfm?fuseaction=document&documentid=60

CHAPTER 27

Accountability

> "It is not only what we do,
> but also what we do not do,
> for which we are accountable." —*Molière*

Imagine public schools that close if kids don't learn, or taxpayer moneys are being misused. Contrary to what some think, such public schools exist. They are called charter schools.

The magic recipe of education, children, and taxpayer funding requires a healthy dash of accountability. When we entrust our children and our wallets to our schools we expect assurances of outcome. Charter schools are granted autonomy to innovate and educate on two specific conditions: fiscal responsibility and academic achievement. If a charter fails in any of these two areas, it may lose its right to stay in business. These schools are held accountable in a multitiered system to assure proper return on investment for taxpayer dollars to our children.

Charter schools are held accountable to the parents

Charter school parents are a choosy bunch who carefully research and select education for their children. If a family is dissatisfied with the academic achievements they are very likely to cash their chips in and move on. The same families are likely to sing the praises of education that fulfill the commitment of proper teaching.

Learning and spending is held accountable by the governing board

The charter operating council hires the management, which in turn employs the school staff. The director answers to the school board on academic development, whereas a business manager and/or treasurer reports on finances.

The governing board reports to the charter school authorizer

The charter sponsor does not only approve the school's right to open, but continues to hold the charter responsible for keeping its goals and commitments. Charters need renewal every so many years (varying based on local rules). The charter governing board must answer to the authorizer on how well the kids are learning and sound financial practices. A charter school that is not performing at desirable levels or is in debt is at risk of nonrenewal (*see chapter 25 and 32*).

Charter schools answer to its lenders

Lenders expect payments on time and in full. If a charter school is delinquent there are consequences in forms of financial penalties, and if needed, the loan is called.

In fact, charter schools are held to a higher standard than most other schools. Because of the element of taxpayer funding there are several government agencies that keep close tabs on performance and fiscal responsibilities. A school that does not educate does not deserve to continue to teach. A business that acts irresponsibly with entrusted funds should be closed down.

Quality assurance is important for all parties involved and taken seriously. There are annual reports on charter school accountability, as well as evaluations of management organizations. The Center for Education Reform continues to call for stronger laws for charter schools, as accountability is an important part of success.

Several charter schools across the nation are also in the practice of having another layer of answerability—the school accountability committee (SAC). It is a group that collects data and provides analysis for reporting to the governing board, authorizer, community, and state. This information is also used by the school to make sure it is true to its mission.

This is a sample description of responsibilities for a charter school SAC:

1. To make recommendations to the administration for assessment of theeducational program, student achievement, and staff, parent, and student satisfaction.

2. To make recommendations to the administration for establishing goals for improvement based on the needs assessment and consistent with the mission and goals of the school.

3. To monitor the progress made toward meeting the improvement goals.

4. To solicit input from staff, parents during all phases of assessment, plan development, implementation, and evaluation.

5. To submit an annual report to the Board of Directors and the District, and make it available to the public.

6. To recommend to the Executive Principal representatives from the school Accountability Committee, other than the principal, to serve on the District Accountability Committee and the District Parent Council.

7. Adopt goals, monitor progress, and report results in a manner consistent with state statutes and policies.

8. To determine a meeting schedule and publish time, date, and location of meetings with all meetings open to the public.

9. To nominate a budget subcommittee to review the annual school budget in terms of alignment with the strategic plan.

Part 7
And There Is More...

In Part 7:

28. My State and Charter School Law
    Does your state have charter school laws? What you can do to impact charter school legislation
29. The Neutral Charter Schools
    Why charter schools are politically unbiased
30. Lingo
    Creaming, handpicking, and other odd terms
31. Starting a New Charter School
    Is your school district in need of a new public school option? Stories and advice from real people that started charter schools
32. When Charter Schools Fail
    Addressing unsuccessful ventures: Why some charters don't make it, how often does it happen, and what do we do now?
33. When Charter Schools Succeed
    The wonder of alternative public education done well

What do cream and cherries have to do with charter schools? Very little, unless it's a fundraiser sundae.

> **OVERVIEW**
>
> Part 7 includes a small directory of odd terms that circulate in charter school debates, as well as additional information about charter school law, advice from charter founders, and questions about charters that go out of business.

CHAPTER 28

My State and Charter School Law

I am one of many parents with a passion for charter schools. Don't judge. Loving charter schools is legal in forty states (plus the District of Columbia and Puerto Rico).

Before we embark on this chapter I need to disclose my lack of expertise on laws of any kind. I am a parent—a charter school mama—not a legislative "edu-Yoda" with copious experience at the state capitol. This book does not constitute as legal advice of any form.

There are bountiful resources on charter school law through your state education department, charter school organizations, libraries, and Web sites (*see end of this chapter as well as index*). This chapter will just cover the basic need-to-knows, and will focus more on why and how parents should concern themselves with what is going as far as education legislation goes. For parents like me, who are concerned about the education of my children, being aware of laws that affect our schools is an important piece of the charter school puzzle.

First, let's start with the federal picture. The mission of the U.S. Department of Education (ED) is to "promote student achievement and preparation for global competitiveness by fostering educational excellence and ensuring equal access." The Education Department's staff establishes financial aid policies for education, and distributes and monitors such funding. ED is also responsible for collecting and publishing research data on U.S. schools and generating national awareness of current educational issues. Another priority for the Education Department is to prevent discrimination and ensure equal and fair access to education for all children in our country.

Title 1 No Child Left Behind (NCLB) was passed in 2001 by President George W. Bush and was founded on four basic "pillars":
- Accountability
- Do what scientific research proves successful
- More parental options in education
- More local control and flexibility

NCLB law was created to provide certain consistencies in public education throughout our nation. Since charter schools are indeed public schools, they too have specific criteria to meet through this legislation. NCLB requires, for example, that all charter school teachers are "highly qualified" and provide rules to how to determine this to be the case.

Since education issues truly belong primarily to state and local governments, the purpose of federal law is to provide the framework and prevent discrepancies, should they occur and encourage replication of existing success.

A fine example of state and federal government collaborative efforts is indeed our charter schools. Minnesota was the first state to pass charter school law in 1991 and soon thereafter parents began exercising the options of creating and operating publicly funded innovative schools. ED researched and distributed the data about these schools performance and soon the (then) U.S. president Bill Clinton encouraged "all states to form charter school law." (See Ed.gov) ED also began offering start-up grants through the Charter Schools Program (CSP) to encourage openings of such schools.

Before you can start opening charter schools, your state must have a charter school law. The ten states that (to date) do not have such law are: Alabama, Kentucky, Maine, Montana, Nebraska, North Dakota, South Dakota, Vermont, Washington, and West Virginia. If you live in any of these states, don't give up! Stay with this chapter, as it will provide a few clues as to how you can personally be instrumental in changing this.

Typically a charter school law is born when a few supportive leaders draft legislation to permit such schools to be produced. However, not all charter school law is created equal, and the quality of such state law tends to be reflective in the successes or failures of charter schools within that state (see Web sites at the end of this chapter for information about charter school law specific to your state).

The Center for Education Reform (CER) conducts charter school specific research and provides reports on the number of schools that close and the factors that contribute to both achievement and hardship (*see chapter 32*). Briefly, here are some of the reasons given:

- Charter school cap: States that do not prohibit charter school growth by limiting the number of schools that can open tend to do better. A more diverse collection of charter schools is also a key factor, as poorly written charter law would hinder certain types of charter schools from creation.

- Options of charter school authorizers: Laws written to permit more than one type of charter school authorizer provide alternatives for charter school founders and encourage expansion of charter schools. Multiple authorizers also provide an effective appeal if you do not find a healthy working relationship with a particular charter authorizing entity.

- Autonomy: A healthy practice in charter school law is to exempt such schools from many state regulations that may slow innovation or prevent distinction between schools. No school, of course, is excused from following federal law, such as civil rights law. However, flexibility is a key component of a successful charter school as it allows for innovation and greater accountability and, as proven, great educational success. By allowing charter schools to be their own legal entity, they can purchase school facilities and control employment decisions. States that permit school districts to include charter school facility costs in local bond elections also save taxpayers money. Remember, charter schools are public schools that are funded by public dollars, so it is important they have access to public financing, which allows them to access funding at a cheaper rate. It does not make sense for one public school to have the ability to bond at one rate whereas another public school around the block has to pay more for building facilities.

- Funding: States and districts should not withhold money from its charter schools for fees and "administrative costs" (charter schools have their administration in-house). While charter schools are public schools, they also operate in many respects as independent entities in areas such as establishing curriculum, administrative staff, and budgeting. Since charter schools operate independently in their finances, they need to be the entity in charge of their finances in order to operate smoothly. Charter schools are public schools and are entitled to fair funding.

CER produces analysis of each state's charter school law and ranks them both in order of strength as well as gives them a report card. Visit the CER Web site at www.edreform.com for up to additional information.

Now that you know what charter school laws does, let's talk about why you—the parent—should concern yourself with it.

I think Pam Benigno, the Education Policy Center Director for the Independence Institute, said it well, "If you don't have it [charter school law], you should fight for it. If you have it, don't take it for granted—during the wrong circumstances it could be taken away."

She is absolutely right. If you live in a state that does not have charter school law, keep in mind that neither did other states just until a short time ago. Charter school law is always instigated by one or several people. Why couldn't that person be you? Recruit a few like-minded friends and connect with your elected leaders at the state capitol. Most legislators are interested in speaking with people who take the time and interest in contacting them. These professionals are most accessible when the legislature is not in session, as they are otherwise busy representing your state's interests in the house or senate.

Pam Benigno often speaks to parent groups about education advocacy. We will elaborate a bit on some of her wise recommendations for parents when advocating for or against education or state public policy. Some of these points overlap with the chapter on networking:

- Exercise your right at the ballot box: Attend town hall and "meet the candidates" meetings, and interview persons who want to serve as you area's elected officials. Be an informed voter. Campaign for charter school friendly officials. And of course—VOTE!

- Organize: The larger the group, the louder the voice. Connect with other charter schools and their families, or in the case of nonexistent charter schools, align yourself with like-minded individuals. Do not underestimate the power of grassroots action. A friend recently told me that elected officials will often listen more to a parent speaking of real life experiences, than someone who is from a paid interest group (no offense if you are from a paid interest group).

- Stay connected: Use the Internet to start an online group, blogs, forums, and other social networks.

- Show respect: Most elected leaders really want to represent well and do a good job. Even if you disagree, be respectful. * I have a little confession to make. I wrote one angry blog once. It's not my style, but I got really worked up. Not only did I type it, I also e-mailed it to the person I was upset with. This legislator deserves copious credit as he took the time to meet with me over coffee as a response. Is he now a cheerleader for charter schools? No. But we had a reasonable discussion and we agreed to disagree. I still feel remorse over that blog entry. There must have been a million more effective ways to express myself…

- Knowledge is power: Take an interest in education and politics and stay abreast of current events. Your search engine will let you subscribe to articles using certain key- words. Enter the words *charter schools* and you can receive daily articles that are written around the nation on your favorite education topic.

- Develop your influence: Serve on district and school committees. Run for office if you have the time and interest. Local school boards, city councils, and county commissioners often have great influence over decisions that may affect your charter school. Remember, local schools are most influenced by locally elected officials. Join the team if you feel that your hometown or county needs to move in a certain direction. At the very least get to know the elected officials serving on your board. They are accessible and can often be reached by simply picking up the phone. Most will appreciate the time you took in sharing your opinion. Support officials who support you. During elections offer to put up a sign and talk to your friends and neighbors. Be visible: attend meetings, conferences, and networking sessions both at school and district level, as well as more global events.

- Listen: Ask questions, learn, read, and verify the information.

- Do the research: Venting emotions may have a time and place, but before you suggest policy changes make sure you have all the facts and that they are indeed facts.

- Be wise: Ask for everything in writing.

- Develop your own credibility: Take time to cultivate integrity as an individual and as a group.

- Be bipartisan: Drop all your predispositions about parties and elected officials. Support for charter schools does not recognize affiliations, and you may hurt your efforts if making assumptions.

- Don't get discouraged: I wish I could tell you everyone is a supporter of charter schools, but that would not be the truth. If you run into a snag, it's a speed bump, not a roadblock. You have the facts on your side and its likely there are more people supporting you than not.

- Learn from others: Seek counsel from the experts. There are wonderful, experienced individuals and organizations available throughout our country. They are wonderful in sharing wisdom that they have accumulated over the years with people who are just starting out. Check out the resource index of this book as well as the acknowledgment section, and you will find a list of wonderful resources that we all continue to learn from.

As an example of the last point: This chapter could not possibly have been written without the help of information through the U.S. Department of Education, Colorado League of Charter Schools, the Center for Education Reform, Pam Benigno, the Independence Institute, and a group of knowledgeable individuals for proofreading (listed in the acknowledgements).

Just as important, stay in touch with federal legislation as well. Subscribe to advocacy network updates through organizations like the National Alliance for Public Charter Schools www.publiccharters.org to stay informed and up-to-date. These groups send out action alerts when your voice or e-mails are needed for charter schools at a national level—simple and efficient.

Remember, you may be viewed as the Rosa Parks of charter schools in your area, but that is a compliment! Rosa Parks was one smart, strong individual who became an instrumental part for much needed change that our nation is still benefiting from.

For more information, please visit the following Web sites:
    U.S. Department of Education: www.ed.gov
    Colorado League of Charter Schools: www.coloradoleague.org
    The Center for Education Reform: www.edreform.com
    The Independence Institute: www.i2i.org

CHAPTER 29

The Neutral Charter Schools

Politics and religion are those two subjects that can divide the most cohesive groups. And surprise, surprise—not everyone agrees when it comes to education.

But regardless of personal political, faith, and education preferences, we can all agree that we desire quality education for our kids. Naturally we will have different opinions and approaches in how we achieve such a goal within our schools, but that's the beauty of school choice. By embracing diversity in school options and working together as a nation, we are far more likely to find effective solutions than to attempt to convert the masses to agree with one method of schooling.

Charter schools offer the perfect environment for doing exactly this. No two charter schools are exactly the same. Each is designed with a specific vision with local flavor. Charter schools embody the vision of variations within public education.

There has been an on-again, off-again rumor that charter schools have religious affiliations. As with most charter school lore of the rumor mill, this is a false claim. Charter schools are public schools, not private schools, and have no religious affiliation. Sure, there are folks who attend charters with various personal faiths, just like in any other type of school. Keeping religion and public schools separate is not overly complicated, since the church is not funding the school and the school is not funding the church.

When it comes to politics though, it's a different story. Public education is funded by the government, and the government is composed of elected officials who represent political parties. It is keeping partisan politics out of the classroom that can present more of a challenge than the other topics. But the focus in education needs to be only on the child and whether or not the child is learning. Adult complications of special interests should not be included. Education is—and should always be—child centered. Last time I checked, all major American political platforms believed in good education.

Besides, in an era when charter schools are bridging the divide of political partisanship in discussions for school choice and innovation of our public schools, there are more reasons to agree than disagree.

Here are some of the benefits our local and national leaders tout for public charter schools:

- Ability to innovate: With fewer regulations, charter schools are able to attempt new approaches in education with increased ease.

- Public charter schools offer school choice for everyone regardless of income, as they are tuition free. If charter schools did not exist, school choice would be an exclusive right for the select few who could afford private schools or have the right situation for homeschooling.

- Charters offer unique explorative programming, which places learning diversity within the public school offering.

- Quality charter schools exist in both suburban and inner-city areas, proving that public schools can take on a chameleon-like characteristic to successfully meet different needs.

- Parental involvement and active family partnership with the school.

- Fewer government regulations simplify the process when a parent or community member wants to directly contribute to education through a charter.

- School choice within the public school system, which drives up overall quality by friendly competition. The winner is the student.

- Charters cost the taxpayer less money because they do not operate with huge overhead. Two layers of an organization are fewer than four (like the public schools of old).

- These schools offer alternatives outside of the neighborhood school of default. It adds to the varied culture of education options, which should be offered, not mandated.

- Charters offer innovative tools and programming that reach students that may otherwise not be served by other education offerings.

- Charter schools are the entrepreneurial educators dream, as each runs like a small, fairly independent business.

- Performance pay.

- Freedom to hire teachers and staff outside the "ordinary" pool.

- Teachers are not required to join the union.*

*Let's briefly touch on the sensitive union topic.

The issue of the organized teachers' union is the elephant in the charter school classroom, so to speak. There are a lot of strong feelings for or against unions in general, so if you suspect that this chapter will upset you, skip on ahead to chapter 30.

As mentioned in chapter 2, charter schools were originally encouraged by the American Federation of Teachers (AFT) president, Al Shanker. He had a vision of charter schools as teacher-led laboratories that would have the freedom to experiment with new practices. The most successful results from Shanker's imagined charter schools would then be transferred to the neighborhood counterparts.

The union founder also anticipated charter schools as a way to empower teachers and encourage innovation and risk-taking. However, as state charter school law began to crop up, one of the options charter schools could exercise as part of their autonomy was not to invite the union to organize the teachers.

Shanker's hopes for charter schools began to take place with empowered teachers, innovation, and risk taking, but without involvement of the very organization he so believed in—the teachers union. It was about the time this began to start place that Shanker's support for charter schools faded.

To date, the majority of charter schools has chosen not to include the teachers union. The reasons given are many and they range, depending on who you ask. Some feel that the union would inhibit the charter school's ability to innovate at the rate independent staff would; others state that the union's tenure practices would prevent the charter's right to excuse inefficient teachers in a timely manner, while a number of individuals expressed doubt that organized teacher representation is necessary or even a viable solution in an environment in which kids (not teachers) should be in front and center.

Yet, there are a few charter schools in which the teachers have invited the union and have organized as a result. The latest such examples are three Civatas Schools in Chicago and two KIPP schools in New York. The union is certainly not saying "no thank you" to added members, and the language about charter schools on the organization's Web site has also been updated to reflect Al Shanker's original hopes for these schools.

There is also a new breed of charter schools popping up, which purposefully include unionized teachers as a part of the plan. Green Dot, for example, is one chain of such schools. When speaking to Green Dot, it was relayed that the goal is truly to be an educational test lab of sorts to try innovative methods that could later be introduced to the traditional public schools. Since those schools have teachers who are organized under union contracts, so do Green Dot schools.

Sure, it's "union-lite," and it does not include all the same components as some of the more traditional, collective bargaining agreements. However, by being a charter school, Green Dot has the opportunity to experiment with different nuances of its union agreement to find a good balance. The Web site for Green Dot Public Schools confirms this philosophy as it reads:

"With Green Dot's success to date, we are demonstrating that public schools can do a far better job of educating students if they are operated more effectively."

The United Federation of Teachers (UFT) has also opened its own chain of charter schools in the New York area. Why do I bring all this up? Because the topic of unions and charters carry historic contentions and political undertones. But clearly there are both charter schools that do have unions and those that don't. This book is not about one type of charter schools, but all.

Teachers unions are in business to serve the teachers (as the organization's name suggests). Parents seek teachers to serve their kids. As long as the teachers are effective in doing their job, there are few parents who care if that's a union card or a frequent visitor's card to the local coffee shop in the professional's wallet. It is then a personal choice for the teacher.

In general, parents are also very concerned that their child's teachers are respected and well treated—regardless of club memberships. To a parent, the teachers union may be the equivalent of what school buses are to teachers. As long as this is the student comes to school on time the teacher could care less if the kid travels by bus, mom's van, or by pogo stick. But if the student is always tardy because the school bus was slowing him down, we have a problem. For a parent, if a student is thriving academically there is little thought as to whether or not the teacher is paying union dues. But if the union becomes the obstacle between the child and a good education, watch out…

The same goes for unions and charter school issues in our communities. Many charter school folks would happily coexist with schools that choose union affiliations as long as such memberships are not expected for all schools. It is when a union opposes propositions that would benefit charter schools that there is a conflict. Such situations become even more laced with spins and turns when the union is involved behind the scenes of the political world of opposing charter school friendly plans, while serving teachers in charter schools in those areas. Such a tangled web…

Personally I think adults often have the education pyramid upside down. Education is about the kids. Teachers support the kids. Unions support teachers. If we want to see efficient improvement in education, we need to focus on what is good for the kids. This should also improve things for the teachers, which in turn should be fine with the unions or any other organization that represents them (pushing my rose-colored goggles up on my nose).

Really, whether we are discussing political parties, unions, or faith-based affiliations, none of these should be an obstacle in assuring fair and equal access to quality education for all children.

The adults need to put themselves and their issues aside, and think of whom our schools' true concern is (you guessed it)—the kids!

Conclusion

The benefits of charter schools quoted above are provided without political symbol next to it. Charter school supporters from both sides may hold each of those views and labeling what is typical would just feed into stereotypes. Regardless of what you and I feel as our personal political convictions, the classroom should be maintained as a neutral zone.

We pay taxes to fund national education. The question should not be whether our moneys provide education but *quality* education. Have you ever heard of someone saying they want to pay taxes without reason or benefits? I'm guessing no. Instead of asking if your area has public schools, you should ask if you have quality public schools. And rather than asking if there are school choice offerings, the question to ask is if there are excellent school choice offerings. We should expect our taxes to support a functioning education system for all students in our community. It is the return on investment on our education tax dollar.

There are both successful and failing schools of all flavors. If we eradicate one type of education we will lose both good and bad, and still not solve the problem. Instead we would be stuck with a goody bag of same mixed results from only one vendor. The focus should instead be on shedding failure and rewarding success throughout school options.

A 2008 article written by Dana Goldstein in *The American Prospect* compared education strategies and results from the United States, one of the lowest performers of the developed countries, and Finland, the leading nation in the same reports. Here is a key quote:

"In the United States, the education debate has been framed as a zero-sum game. But a look at Finland, whose schools rank No. 1 in global surveys, shows that a *national* commitment to education can neutralize political debates over school reform."

You should also know that school choice and merit pay is alive and well in Finland.

The U.S. Department of Education's mission is to assure fair and equal access to quality education. Proper schooling is a civil rights issue for our children, not a political platform.

Lastly, kids are not politically partial. Ask them what they think of a school that keeps their family involved in their educational environment, employs teachers who are sincerely involved in their success, offers them respect, believes in them, and teaches them.

Kids do not mind if you call it a traditional, private, or charter school, nor if a liberal or conservative adult made them possible. They care about whether or not it's available to them—and charter schools are.

We can learn a lot from our kid's perspective.

For more information, visit the following Web sites:
    www.greendot.org
    www.uft.org
    www.aft.org
    www.prospect.org/cs/articles?article=no_education_silver_bullet

CHAPTER 30

Lingo

> **Chapter Facts:**
> **Active Ingredient:** **Purpose:**
> Clarification of charter school myths and terms (1mg)..................To inform and educate
>
> *Uses:* Correct information and fact sources may prevent responses like:
> - confusion
> - headaches
> - nausea, heartburn, indigestion, upset stomach, and diarrhea
> - blowing your top
> - tongue-tied frustration
> - anger
> - depression
>
> *Warnings:*
> If you are exposed to one or more negative comments per day about charter schools, you may need to change your peer group or see your doctor (he or she may be a better friend than those other guys. Besides, the doctor has to listen. You're paying for the visit). Frequent or long-term exposure to unsupportive remarks about your child's school may build resentment toward the speaker, hypersensitivity, and/or activism.
>
> **Do not use:**
> With any other products unless you are absolutely certain they contain the truth—and nothing but the truth—about charter schools.
>
> **Stop use and ask your supporting charter organization if:**
> - new symptoms occur
> - redness and swelling are present
> - you are still confused beyond belief
>
> These signs could be symptoms of a serious condition called denial, or worse, weak state charter school laws.
>
> **If you are pregnant or breastfeeding** you shall not proceed before reading "How to enroll your embryo in a charter school."
>
> *Keep within reach of children.*
>
> **Overdose warning:** Reading this chapter more than once may cause the growth of the cerebral cortex and vertebrae column, both which may be powerful when acting as your child's school advocate. In other words, you may make critics of school choice look bad.

Charter schools have its own language. No, it's not like pig latin. The language consists of phrases and comments that refer to charter schools and their practices. Most commonly you will hear these words from someone who does not like charter schools or, more often, simply uninformed about how charter schools function.

This guide should come in handy to help you in correcting inaccurate information and educating your friends and family about common charter school myths.

Creaming:

Answers.com defines the term as:

The yellowish fatty component of unhomogenized milk that tends to accumulate at the surface

The FREE dictionary has the same definition as well as this explanation:

The choicest part: the cream of the crop.

When it comes to public schools of choice, the first definition can hardly be used. I have yet to see a charter school with accumulating fat layers of either money or unnecessary administration.

Instead, *creaming* is a term sometimes hurled at charter schools by its nonsupporters as an attempt to play down the school's successes. The tale goes that the charters achieve such shiny results by simply attracting the highest performing students because they are the best program in town.

Before we begin chatting about this claim, let's clarify a couple of facts—charter schools are public schools and must abide by the same antidiscrimination laws as any other public school. Secondly, the word *creaming* is sometimes incorrectly used interchangeably with the phrase *handpicking*. Technically these are two separate* accusations, and today we are only covering the term *creaming*.

High- and low-quality schools come in all sorts of titles. So to level the playing field let's just take the word *charter* out of the statement and reduce it to its true origin. Do high-quality schools attract *better* students? There is a fundamental problem in labeling anyone better or worse. We all have strengths and weaknesses, and all students are loaded with potential.

But given the choice, the *majority* of families would choose a proven school over the one ridden with problems. It's just human nature. When you're in the produce department, do you gravitate toward the banged-up rotting fruit, or the orchard-fresh selection? Do you read labels or check the expiration date? What if they cost the same to the customer? Which one do you think would fly off the shelves faster? Did the quality product attract the *better* consumer, or just *more satisfied* consumers? Shall we all stock our grocery shelves full of nasty produce just to prove a point? Which point?

Good schools will always be more popular than the bad ones regardless of what "type" of school it is. In an area where neighborhood schools are thriving, property values and home sales tend to do the same. A top-notch private school usually carries a lengthy waiting list. And where there are high-caliber charter schools, you can count on a whole lot of families filling out enrollment forms.

In conclusion, the word *creaming* is a weird form of a backhanded compliment. So the next time someone says your school is *creaming* (translated: the more popular choice as it is a quality school) practice this new reply, "Well, thank you." You may need to follow up with the explanation above.

Cherry-picking (or handpicking):

Critics say charter schools show such promise and shiny results because they cherry-pick their students. *Do they?* Of course not! They let my kids in.

All joking aside, charter schools, by law, cannot choose their students. Charter schools are public schools and must follow the same antidiscrimination laws as everyone else.

Charter schools usually admit students using either a first-come-first-served policy or lottery system (see charter school enrollment). There may be a few variances for siblings and children of school staff, but none of these policies permit enrollment based on gender, ethnicity, country of origin, or even abilities.

And no, there is no charter school litmus test. Charter schools admit anyone. Charter schools do well because they teach their students well. Period.

Have I heard of families accepting charter enrollment for an older child so that a sibling can get in? Yes. Have I heard of someone seeking employment at a charter school in an effort of assuring enrollment for their child? Yes. Have I ever known of a charter school tipping the scales in favor of a family due to status, bribes, or threats? Never!

Draining:

There is this urban legend that charter schools are draining public funds from the district schools.

State and federal funding—per pupil revenue (PPR)—follows the student. But doesn't that just plain make sense? Isn't it the school that our student attends that actually pays for the expense of educating the kid?

It would make no sense to pay schools for students who are enrolled elsewhere. The only solution to have all funding go to one single school would be to only have *one school for all the kids in the state.*

Boy! That would sure save us a lot of money. I can see it now: hundreds of thousands of kids filing single line into an education superdome to be schooled by one teacher at the fifty-yard line. It would certainly solve that all state, federal, local tax, grants, and donations went to the same facility. That would be a swell idea if education quality was not an issue. But good education is not possible if the good of the child is not being considered.

Truth is that a charter school does not take away from a neighborhood school any more than the neighborhood school takes away from the charter school. There are state funding inequities that are sometimes more favorable toward the neighborhood school, but that is no fault of the kids that attend the traditional schools.

White/Black Flight:

This is probably the most offensive term in existence that is used by some to describe the charter school movement. To reduce families who opt for alternative public education to skin color is simply appalling.

The term *white flight* describes the demographics of Caucasians who move from urban neighborhoods to the suburbs. *Black flight* is the term for the African American counterpart. Neither phrase originates from the charter school movement. Instead, *white flight* stems from the years following World War II when many Caucasian Americans left the cities to suburban communities. It was a time when exclusionary covenants and redlining of neighborhoods still took place. *Black flight* is a more recent term.

There has been a parallel drawn between charter schools and suburbs. The suburban communities attract home buyers with new housing stock, planned neighborhoods, open spaces, schools, parks, recreation, and a family friendly atmosphere. Some are also drawn to these communities due to lower crime rates, less congestion, and more.

Similarly, charter schools offer something different from the mainstream, such as often smaller class sizes, theme-focused curricula, close-knit school relationships, competitive results, and a family friendly atmosphere.

But is selecting a school really racially motivated? In most cases no. Most families who attend option schools do so because that particular education program is the best fit for their child. The black flight label has been stuck on ethnic families who choose schools outside the neighborhood schools. The same goes for Caucasians and the white flight tag. In other words, if you are practicing your parental rights for school choice, you are regarded as a flier by some, regardless of skin tone.

Charter School Cap

Some states have limitations as to how many charter schools can open or operate. This is paralyzing to the supply and demand within the movement, as charter's increasing popularity among parents far outweigh the availability of such schools.

Of forty states that offer charter schools, twenty-six have limitations on how many charters are permitted to operate. Since most charter schools are enrolled to capacity and have long waiting lists, these state caps stand in the way of offering public school choice to thousands of kids across the country.

Charter Tuition

Charter schools are public schools and funded by the taxpayer. ***There is no tuition for charter schools.***

Charter School Litmus Test

Charter schools are public schools and do not administer a litmus test. See enrollment policies and exceptions.

Cash Cow

A renowned charter school critic, who called charter schools "cash cows," recently visited one of my blogs. At first I chalked it up to one rare instance, but before I knew it I heard the claim again. So unknowing how common this phrase is, we should probably cover it.

The critic referred to charter schools as "cash cows" for profiting companies and billionaire philanthropists. Is this true? First of all, charter schools on average are funded at 61% of a traditional public school. Since many school districts are stating that they are underfunded, then how can any business be getting rich from schools receiving almost 40% less funding?

And please let this be a shout-out to the billionaire philanthropists who supplement funding to our charters through grants and donations. These men and women did not and are not making their fortune off of charter schools but giving money to them. We are so lucky to have financially successful individuals in this country who have a conviction for education and are willing to donate money and resources to their cause.

It should also be added that most philanthropic dollars to U.S. charter schools come through grants, and not accessible to every school and every purpose. In other words, grants don't show up in a ginormous blank check.

Kindergarten bandits

This term is a combination of handpicking, creaming, and draining. In other words, do charter schools set out to cherry-pick the highest performing kindergarten students, then leave the district schools hemorrhaging cash due to lack of enrollment and poor test results? By the way, how does one know which kindergartener will become a high performing student?

See handpicking, creaming, and draining, as well as chapter 21 "Charter School Enrollment."

CHAPTER 31

Starting a New Charter School

So you want to start a charter school. Maybe there aren't any in your area, or perhaps the one you have your eye on is at capacity with a lengthy waiting list. Or do you have a group of like-minded individuals who have a great idea for a school that will complement the existing assortment of public schools?

What do you need to know before taking on the endeavor of starting a new charter school? We will not go very deeply into the subject as you will need a whole lot more information than one chapter can hold. There are plenty of resources on the topic both on the Internet, in your library, and with your state charter organization.

Instead we have a few highlights of what to consider and advice from charter school veterans who once were pioneers like you!

Surround yourself with good people:

It may not be as hard as it sounds. If you and your original group have a good plan in mind, which is desired by the community, you will soon find a following. You personally do not need to be a jack-of-all-trades and a master-of-all. If that's the case you are spreading yourself too thin anyway.

You will need administrators, educators, visionaries, legal advice, money folks, researchers, and more. If you don't find these specialties among yourselves, hire out (by conventional methods or check into EMO and CMO services).

Connect with your state and local charter organizations:

These folks are equipped with tools and answers, which you will need through the charter school-starting process and beyond. Charter school organizations are designed to assist charter schools in achieving success through providing information, resources, and services specifically for these entities. Check your state education Web site for more information.

Do your homework:

Before making the commitment of taking on such an endeavor, take the time to do the research. Learn the demographics of the area(s) of geographic interest for the prospective school: Is the community welcoming to charter schools? What schools (charter and noncharters) already exist? How well are the other schools doing? What is the per pupil revenue? What are area families looking for? What will make your school unique? And so on.

Go sightseeing:

You'll be enrolling real kids in a real charter school, right? Then it's important that you see some in action. If you thought that existing, successful charter schools would snub their nose at you and tell you to find your own way, you will likely find the opposite.

Every charter school is in existence thanks to thousands of hours of dedication. The individuals behind the schools are usually very welcoming to others who share their passion for charter schools and enjoy talking about their school "back in the days…"

Take a tour of as many charter schools as you can. Visit schools with similar demographics and scope as the one you are considering, but also stop by at least one or two that are different, just to get a sense of comparison. If you have not been to traditional and private schools in the area, visiting these schools may also be valuable. Sure, you may have made your mind up about the other type of schools without setting foot in one. There are people who have done the same about charter schools. But is it the right approach?

By visiting the other schools you are showing an active interest in the community beyond your own education project, opening communications that cross the boundaries of "us-and-them," and signaling that you are a public school team player. Who knows? You may end up learning something unexpectedly positive from your visit.

Ask the charter operators what worked and what would they never try again. Keep a log of names and contact information. You'll never know when you'll need that again.

Network:

Attend charter school conferences, meetings, and organizational events. These are folks you don't just need to know, but you'll want to know.

Scope locations [*plural*]:

Plenty of charter schools do not end in the original location in mind due to varying circumstances. Perhaps the authorizer is friendlier toward charters somewhere else, the majority of interested families live in the opposite end of town, you can't find affordable space where you were hoping, or an all-around better opportunity opens up in a new location. Keep your options open and have plan B, C and D in mind.

And of course…the money:

Talk to your state charter organization about funding and the minimum number of students you should have to start a school. Leaders in Alaska, for example, are working to change a law that penalizes charters financially when enrollment is below one hundred students.

Write a list of priorities. Unfortunately, it is unlikely that you'll be able to be the highest bidder for teacher pay, cutting-edge technology, low student to teacher ratios, a complete and permanent building—all in the beginning.

Few charter schools open without an initial start-up grant. Talk to your state charter school organization and state education department about what options may be viable for you. *Read more in chapter 26.*

Get political:

I know (eye roll), you're not political and neither should schools be. Maybe in a perfect world, but as a charter school founder wannabe you will need to interact with various government agencies, many of which are political.

School districts are the most common form of charter school authorizers. District boards are composed of local elected officials. The same is true for some of the city and state governments, which you may need to contact for various steps in the process. Getting your charter application approved by the authorizer will take a majority vote from its board. Not everyone is in favor of charter schools. The good news is that charter schools are increasingly a bipartisan issue.

If the thought of politics makes your tongue swell up and break out in a rash, think of it as relationship building or sales. That's far less intimidating. You have a good product, right? Now you are selling your concept to the board.

The time factor

Starting a school takes time and dedication, and it is not for the faint of heart. Keep in consideration that hundreds of volunteer hours are typically involved in a charter school prior to opening its doors. If there is one charter school that was opened without ever running into an objection or obstacle, it certainly was not interviewed for this book. It is overcoming these hurdles that may make or break the venture. Charter schools are started and operated by driven people who interpret the word *no* as *try again*.

Keep your eye on the prize

Patience is a virtue. Never lose sight of the goal in mind, and envision the "who's" and "why's" you are doing this for along the way. There will be good days and bad. Progress may be better suited from a bird's-eye perspective than individual tasks for motivation purposes. Keep in mind: Rome was not built in one day; neither will your charter school be.

Is all aboard? Take all above in consideration and then consider your family situation. Starting a charter school is a serious endeavor. Does your family share this dream, and will your spouse be supportive? After all, many founders start charter schools because of their family. Just make sure your family is clear on what that entails.

"When I was asked about what it takes to start a charter school, I paused, laughed, and said, 'To someone asking, I say RUN!' After controlling myself, I gave it some thought. What are the key ingredients in starting a successful charter school? That's a large question, but in short it takes dedication, strong vision, detailed planning, networking, asking never-ending questions, resourcefulness, creativity, a plethora of time and energy, and a group of like-minded, do-what-it takes volunteers who are willing to go above and beyond to get it done, understanding, and support from your family! The hours and commitment are grueling as we've discussed, and without a supportive, understanding hubby, I would have had to really scale back or quit altogether considering the time I was putting in.

Then comes the part about finding the right administrative leader who can take the years of planning and dedication, put the vision into action while solidifying the foundation before beginning to pour the walls, and strengthen what is happening within them.

The planning stage is thankless, burning the midnight oil night after night...but in the end, if it's done right, it is one of the most amazing accomplishments! To walk into a school that is thriving and successful due in part to the years of work behind the scenes is chilling. The positive affect that you have the opportunity to have on the hundreds of children who walk through the doors every day is astounding. To hear parents rave about their child's charter school and how it has helped them, gone above and beyond, and how much their child is learning, makes it all worth it!"

—*Lorrie Grove, cofounder of North Star Academy (CO)*

"I have worked at three start-up schools in six years here in Utah. Previous to that, I started up a county and district-level School Readiness program in rural northern California and was involved in a start-up year for a traditional elementary school in Salinas, CA. I also worked in political polling and survey research for about five years, starting up an office in Eugene, OR. You could say I like the excitement and energy of a start-up. I have had the greatest experience of my life opening the schools and then being involved at the state level with the chance to meet and learn from folks at the national level. It has been a great six years! I believe the following concepts are key for establishing a charter school:

(1) If you don't have the energy, don't bother. So much is required of every person involved, from writing the application, to enrollment, to opening the doors, and beyond. Sometimes all you have is the ability to muscle through to the next level.

(2) If you are not willing to sacrifice everything for a year or more, don't bother. Founders must not rest on preopening efforts. Be committed for the long haul.

(3) Don't be guilty of undermining efforts to realize the founding vision by paid personnel. Working and serving together will create a powerful cultural foundation for the school that is imperative.

(4) Understand no one person has it all figured out. Get help from those who have gone before. Hurdles happen at every step—learn from them and make the school stronger.

(5) Finally, it is all about student achievement. Period. There is no room for hidden agendas or petty grievances. If it is about anything else, start up something else but don't waste the time and effort on a school that pretends. Make the school you envision matter!"

—*Darren Beck, Director, Rockwell Charter High School, UT; President, Utah Association of Public Charter Schools (2007 - 2009); Former Director, The Ranches Academy Public Charter School (2004 - 2008)*

"Five years ago, several professionals committed to online learning concurred with me that there was a significant void in access to online curriculum. Then, online education was only available to dual-parent, single-income suburban families fortunate to be able to provide computer and Internet access, as well as crucial adult supervision and support to their children. However, there are many students, without those home resources, who can benefit from online education. We founded Hope Online with a commitment to serve those students.

By creatively partnering with community organizations, in rural, urban, and suburban areas, Hope Online has established a network of local learning centers that students attend in order to access their online curriculum and the face-to-face adult support that distinguishes Hope Online students' success. These community organizations know their neighborhood and understand the needs of the students. Learning center mentors and directors are able to adapt their practices and level of support to accommodate the circumstances and challenges faced by students from their community.

Students engage in online curriculum because it is relevant to them. At Hope Online, students are given the tools to learn, feel empowered by their accomplishments, and come to believe that academic success and high school graduation are not only a dream, but also a reality that they can achieve.

If you are interested in becoming a HOPE Online Learning Center, know that HOPE Online provides: Funding for each student, a state-of-the art computer lab, a core curriculum, individualized student learning plans, student recruitment support, professional development opportunities, and technical support."—*Heather O'Mara, Chief Executive Officer, Hope Online Learning Academy Co-Op*

"My advice to anyone thinking about starting a charter school is simple: don't do it. Don't do it if you can't work twelve-hour days, withstand withering criticism from parents, teachers, and board members, or are not prepared to delve into the morass of county, state, and federal regulations. Don't do it unless you have a deep love for children, the drive to ensure that each one of them succeeds, the courage to demand excellence from yourself and everyone in your organization every day, the humility to surround yourself with the smartest, most talented people that you can find, and the wisdom to listen to them.

But if you must start a charter school, do it right. Learn from the best charter schools in the country. Develop a deep understanding of how great schools develop their school culture, ensure safety and discipline, use assessment data to drive instruction, recruit and develop teachers, utilize strategic planning, and approach governance. Develop a detailed plan for addressing each of these critical areas with specific goals and outcome measures. You must also be committed to getting better every year. It is a hard business to succeed where so many others have failed, but if you get it right, you will save the lives of hundreds of children. It's worth it."

—*Lyman Millard, Director of Development and Communications for Citizens' Academy (OH), and former Operations Manager and member of Citizens' Academy's founding team*

"Study best practices. There are some excellent schools out there. Visit them. Observe them. We found other school leaders to be very mission-focused and very open to sharing what they have learned.

Hook up with an organization like Building Excellent Schools (www.buildingexcellentschools.org) and consider using their charter school founder-training program.

Find an outstanding school leader, like our Marshall Emerson. He is very focused on the goal line and never takes his eye off of it. He sets the tone for the entire school—teachers and students. He knows his business, he will not waver from it, and he will not add "cute" and "flowery" features that detract from the focus on bringing urban students to grade-level performance, and preparing them for college.

Find a great curriculum person. Again, curriculum must teach the students what they are required to know, by state standards. It must also teach beyond those standards in order to prepare students for college. The curriculum person must know how to assess student comprehension of the material, and must be skilled and creative enough to know how to modify teaching methodology if students are not advancing.

Find mission-driven teachers, teachers who want to be there for the students, teachers who live to see the light in a student's eyes when he or she "gets it," teachers who will do whatever it takes to help a student understand, and teachers who did not go into the profession for the long summer vacations, because those are a thing of the past!"

—*The Leadership of Entrepreneurship Preparatory School (OH)*

"Starting a charter school can be incredibly rewarding because you can bring to life your vision of what a school should be. However, it is also incredibly difficult, as you are essentially creating a small business with its own unique set of regulations and requirements. For some, the challenges of launching a charter school may ultimately outweigh the rewards. For those individuals, there are beginning to be other options. Charter management organizations (CMOs) are networks of charter schools that provide the back-office and instructional supports across multiple sites, taking advantage of the economies of scale. Thus, functions such as purchasing, student information services, and human resources—as well as professional development for teachers and principals—are no longer the responsibility of the single individual (i.e., principal) opening a school. If you've wanted to start a school and be a principal, joining a CMO network may be a way to accomplish that dream and also have a significant support network to back you up."—*Yee-Ann Cho, Chief Executive Officer, Envision Schools (CMO)*

CHAPTER 32

When Charter Schools Fail

This is the chapter none of us wish we need to write. Unfortunately, as with any other area in society, unsuccessful ventures occur. How common are failing charter schools? Why do they fail? Can it be prevented? What happens now?

Firstly, *successful charter schools* far outweigh the ones that aren't. Statistically speaking, 12% of the nation's charter schools have closed.

Todd Ziebarth, Vice President of Policy and Research for the National Alliance for Public Charter Schools, was recently asked how many "lousy" charter schools are too many, to which he answered, "One is too many." One broken school is a problem as it affects children and taxpayers alike, and needs to be taken seriously. We should not be satisfied until we raise the standards for all students; hence substandard programs need to be dealt with swiftly.

Why do successful charter schools care if the few "lousy" charter schools stay open or not? Consider the Jack-in-the-box effect. In the 1990s the fast food chain, Jack in the Box, became infamous as four kids died and six hundred reportedly got ill from eating undercooked hamburgers contaminated with the fecal bacteria E. coli O157:H7. The event was devastating.

The Jack in the Box E.coli reports affected how the general public thought of the chain, food handling, and fast food in general. Soon other fast-food joints began communicating their food safety rules and engaging in self-imposed meat checks. Why? Because Jack in the Box's confirmed crappy burgers tainted the reputation of the entire burger kingdom.

Keep in mind that McDonald's alone is said to serve 4.2 billion hamburgers per day, but it wasn't the consumptions without incident that were of concern—it was the six hundred plus with confirmed problems that made us woozy. If you think about it, if you were one of the individuals who got sick, or the parent of a child who died, would statistics make you feel any better? Of course not. It happened to you, 100%!

Did the burger industry learn a few things from the awful event? You bet your buns. They installed the mentioned safety checks and began improving communications of recall.

The reputation of education in the U.S. is in a similar predicament. We have lousy schools and we have those that are outright fantastic. It is true for all kinds of schools, public and private. However, infamous programs and underperformance give the general public that cautious feeling even though education often happens without scandalous incidents.

It is unlikely that people set out to make people sick with tainted meat, and it is just as doubtful that folks dedicate themselves to education with the intent of failing. Yet food poisoning and unsuccessful schools exist.

Charter schools are no exception. Out of the thousands of charter schools across the nation a percentage does not make the cut, whereas many achieve above expectations. Regardless of the frequency, we cannot face the families of the kids let down by our efforts and say, "it doesn't happen that often." If it happened to your child, it was once too many.

Unlike the food industry and in many instances—the traditional school system—charter schools with problems close down. As said earlier 12% of the nation's charter schools did close. What percentage of traditional schools would close if held to the same standard?

Charter schools are held accountable on many more levels than other public education counterparts. It is a system of high standards set to drive excellence. But when these expectations are not met, charter schools close.

A group of Arizona charter school operators recently assumed the previously volunteer-based state charter school association, and started revamping by calling for enforcement and accountability of their own charter schools. Excellence can be contagious if given the right environment.

So not only do we need to acknowledge past attempts, but also we need to press on by learning from what went wrong, try to learn quickly from past mistakes, and make a plan of problem prevention. The Center for Education Reform (CER) has studied what works and what does not for the past fifteen years. This organization collects data on charter schools and offers many resources to the public about such schools. One of the very helpful documents is the Charter School Accountability Report, which is found through the organization's Web site.

This data reflects time and time again that many of the reasons for closing charter schools can be prevented, especially at the state level. According to the 2009 CER Accountability Report, 41% of the charter school closings were due to financial deficiencies such as low enrollment or funding inequities, 27% of the closed charter schools reported mismanagement, and only 14% closed because the academics were not at acceptable standards. All in all, of the thousands of charter schools that have opened since 1992 (the year before the Jack in the Box event), 657 charters across our nation have closed.

A study of existing charter school success is probably at least as important as the research about failures. *Newsweek* and *US News* are two commercial magazines that report annually on the top schools in the nation. Charter schools are no strangers to these lists and represent more than their statistical presence of charter to traditional ratio for such honors.

What do these schools do that works? What makes them rank among the top? Can it be duplicated? Why don't you look in the index of this book and e-mail a few to ask? They'll be tickled to share their success with anyone interested in the good of education. That's just the kind of people they are.

CER may also hold a piece of the puzzle for charter school success in its accountability report: Charter schools that do well tend to be in states that have strong charter school laws. Where charter schools have the most problems, state legislature needs to provide significant changes (*see chapter 28*).

Granted, perfection in this area may be more of a journey than a destination, although the goal cannot be anything but.

My charter school is at risk of closing. Now what?

Todd Ziebarth of the National Alliance for Public Charter Schools was asked this. The following advice is formed from his response:

The first question you should ask is why. Why is your school at risk of closing? What are the specific issues? Sometimes, being "at risk of closing" means that there are constructive measures that your school can take to avoid it. Do your school's governing council and/or administrator have a plan of action to solve these problems? Can you as a parent contribute to the solution?

Did the charter school authorizer provide a timeline for action items, closing process, or decision making surrounding the decision to whether or not keep the school open? Begin scouting school options. Should the school seize to exist, which school would you consider? Begin your research and don't forget to check open enrollment deadlines.

School closures are awful for everybody; this includes charter schools. Since the charter school authorizer is often seen as the heavy in charter school closures, it may be important to hear what they have to say. This is what charter school sponsors want parents to know about school closures:

SUNY Charter Schools Institute (New York): While we of course hope that no charter school parent has to face this issue, they do need to be aware that it is a possibility. Their best defense is information. As noted above, parents need to understand the renewal process their child's school will undergo and the timing for that process. Parents need to know how the school as a whole is performing on any required state assessments, as well as in relation to the school's own goals. Parents should make it a point to stay informed about how the school is doing in relation to its authorizer's standards for renewal. And when there are problems, parents must stay up-to-date about the proposed solution and its implementation.

POLK County School Board (Florida): The most important thing a parent should know about a charter school closure is that the sponsor and the school's first priority is to transition students quickly and smoothly to an appropriate school setting. While there may be a number of outstanding issues to be resolved, all of those are secondary to assuring that students and their records are placed at a school to assure a seamless transition for each student.

Secondly, while school closures do happen, the process for approving and monitoring charter schools is designed to minimize school closures. In those rare instances when school closures do occur, the resources of the school district are mobilized to assure minimal student disruption. In some cases, a charter school will remain open, at least in the short term, with district staff in place to run the school. In other cases, transportation is arranged for students to attend a local school, or an array of school options is offered to students and their parents. This information is provided to parents in a variety of ways, such as parent information meetings, general information letters and e-mails, as well as student-specific letters and e-mails, which provide individual school options based on the student's address and educational needs.

If a charter school is closed, the sponsor understands that this is a difficult time for everyone. Direct specific questions to the appropriate personnel. If a parent isn't sure who to call, or is not getting the answers he or she needs, call the sponsor's charter school office and ask the question. If no one in the office knows the answer to your question, they can either research that answer and get back to you, or direct your call to someone who can assist you.

Michigan Council of Charter School Authorizers: During the past fifteen years, Michigan authorizers have acted to close approximately thirty charter public schools. These actions have been taken for a variety of reasons, but they all boil down to one central issue: the schools are no longer providing adequate service to the students they serve, or to the taxpayers of the state.

This is the most important role and responsibility an authorizer possesses. Quality oversight means knowing what's working and what isn't; when the school is no longer sustaining an effective operation, it is the authorizer's responsibility to identify the situation and take action. It takes an iron will on the part of the authorizing institution to weather the storm and do what's necessary to safeguard taxpayer dollars and ensure quality education opportunities for kids. The ripple effect is substantial; the authorizer's governing board and institutional leaders will all be tested.

This is one area where Michigan's oversight community has proved its mettle. Once undertaken, these closure decisions are consistently well documented and grounded in fact. Efforts have been made to turn around a school's performance, including clearly articulated plans of correction, one-year "probationary" contracts, and the provision of third-party technical assistance. Each authorizer's governing board has heard all relevant facts before taking a vote on closure, and schools have been given an opportunity to make their case. However, the privilege of holding a charter is just that—

a privilege. In Michigan, where the number of university-granted charters is capped, there is simply no room for low performers.

The Indianapolis Charter Schools Initiative in the Office of the Mayor:
The mayor's office is committed to ensuring that students and families that may be displaced due to charter closing are effectively taken care of. While it is undesirable to close a charter school because of the adverse impact on some kids and families, at times such an action will be required. Ensuring that students and families are taken care of can be accomplished by allowing a different, high-quality charter school to open at the same location, or working with parents to find another school that meets their needs.

Prevention

The type of trouble that can close a charter school does not commonly happen overnight. If insufficient funding is the issue, the budget would have reflected it for some time; mismanagement and lack of learning may also have sprawling symptoms over some time. In addition, there may be times when an authorizer, aware of trouble brewing, will send the charter school with a laundry list of things to do which may remedy the situation.

Sometimes a charter school can overcome these obstacles, improve, and stay operating. Other times the issues may be too difficult to overcome.

Yet there are so many parents who learn about their beloved school's predicament in the eleventh hour. How can you prevent yourself from being that parent? And more importantly, how can you prevent your school from being in this position?

There are obviously no guarantees that certain efforts would change the course a school is going in during the wrong circumstances. However, there are plenty of best practices described throughout this book that you can and should apply. The most powerful defense a parent has is his or her personal involvement in the school. Remember, you don't have to be a board member of the governing council to attend public meetings at your school or at district or state levels.

By making yourself a part of the fabric of your kid's school, you will also gain a good sense of the climate and happenings throughout. Being on a first-name basis with teachers, school leaders, state charter school organizations, and other parents helps you connect and stay abreast of current events. But as part 5 of this book described, it isn't just learning about your school that is important, but being a contributor as well.

So ask yourself if your school needs you, because I am willing to bet that you need your charter school!

CHAPTER 33

When Charter Schools Succeed

I imagine that when Ferdinand Magellan's crew sailed around the world and proved that the earth was indeed round, not flat, there were still plenty of nonbelievers. Here they were trying to tell some of the richest and influential people of the land that they were—wrong! Since people of Magellan's time had been executed for such blasphemy, they must have been really sure to make such claim—or really stupid. I am also convinced that there was a stout sixteenth century politician or two who went to the grave still swearing up and down that the earth was as flat as a stamp.

In education you will find a similar scenario. There are some who will never believe in the successes of charter schools regardless of how much you prove it. They'll claim their sources are better than yours and yaddayadda. Fact is that in most states charter schools teach the kids to read a year or more ahead of the other schools, teach real math, take on kids with various challenges, and help kids graduate who otherwise may not. Charter schools are successful and we're really sure about it.

Just look in the back of this book and you will find a sampling of charter schools that have been recognized on a national level for a job well done. Granted, this book could not fit every wonderful charter school into the allotted page count, so consider it a sampling.

Successful charter schools also experience another symptom—lengthy waiting lists. Parents everywhere are filling out enrollment forms for the top schools in their area and charter schools are among them. This is a sign that we need to open more charter schools, duplicate existing success, and lift any existing limits on the number of charter schools that can operate.

Innovation is not at its peak acceleration if the breaks are on. Word of a quality school spreads among parents at incredible rates. It makes sense as parent satisfaction of public education in general is not impressive. Charter schools are a feather in the cap of public education as they prove that the theory of education that is free to the public can provide strong academics, variation, and can be child centered.

Perhaps most importantly, charter school success does not happen by chance. Through the cohesive relationship of families and educators, charter schools prove time and time again that the success is not only existent—it's persistent. From the lawmakers to the charter school founder, the leadership, and the educators—and of course the families—we each play a contributing role in charter school success.

Part 8
Post Script

31 Flavors of Public Education

Few are the people that don't like ice cream. Perhaps I don't remember meeting any anti-ice cream eaters because "weirdies" get filed in the black hole of my memory. This book is for us "nonweirdies" who have appreciation for cold, sweet, drippy ice cream.

Good schools are just like ice cream. Traditional, magnets, and charters—they are all ice cream—just different in flavors. Our quality school districts are the ice cream parlors where the decadent treats are being offered. During a cone purchase, do you give much thought to what the other guy just bought? Or do you, like me, give little attention to what's sliding down other people's pieholes, read each item on the menu, and savor the imaginary moment of indulgence before placing your order? My friends include ice cream eaters of all flavors. Though we may be different in preference, we respect each other's choices.

Imagine walking up to the counter and having the ice cream man declare that the country is only serving vanilla, because vanilla is a fine flavor that should cater to *all* customers? We would have a national riot on our hands by strawberry, chocolate, and sherbet lovers alike. Vanilla lovers would protest as well since demand for their special treat just went way up, which could cause a shortage and way more spoons in the container.

Many would suck it up and eat vanilla for awhile until that need for a flavor fix really sets in. If the ice cream-diversity ban was local, nonconformists may find themselves willing to travel or make their own. There are other brands of ice cream out there, too. In education we call them private schools. We pay more for a cone at the designer shop, but it is customized with toppings and warm waffle cone choices. Design shops have devoted patrons no matter what the other vendors offer, but imagine how their business would grow if they were the sole providers of flavor options.

A great ice cream parlor caters to the varied needs of its ranging customers with equal appreciation, just like a sound school district is inclusive of the needs of all its students. Have you ever paid for your treat and had some guy hiss at you that your chocolate ice cream purchase is hurting the sales of strawberry custard? Has someone told you they think less of you for not preferring their favorite ice cream? I am going to guess no.

So why do some criticize other families for attending a different kind of school than theirs? Should we expect parents to sacrifice the schooling choice best suited for their kid, because one type of education *should* be fine for all? If we flooded all the kids into one type of public school, what are we really accommodating—the kids' varied needs or some desire to make others conform? Debating which is better, chartered or traditional, is a waste of time. There is ample demand for *all* flavors of public education.

Dear Reader,

I hope you have found this book helpful in learning about charter schools. I would like to encourage you to examine all school choices with the same interest. Remember, school choice is not for the other guy. It's for all of us.

Regardless of which school becomes the choice for your family, I wish you and yours the very best.

And one last special thanks to all who have been a part of making this book. Just like many of our schools, it could not have been done without you!

Sincerely,
Karin Piper
Charter School Mom

Glossary

accountability: Responsibility.
administration: Management.
admission: Admitting someone to enter or enroll.
advocacy: Pursuit of influencing outcome.
advocate: A person who speaks in support of an action or concept.
application: A form.
at-risk student: Someone who is deemed to be at risk of not graduating.
authorizer: Charter school sponsor.
autonomy: Independence.
blog: Online web journal.
board meetings: Meetings of organizational leadership.
bond: Form of funding.
book fee: Cost of textbooks.
brick-and-mortar: Physical facility.
bylaws: Rules adapted by an organization to organize its own affairs.
  car pool: Arranged ride-sharing.
cash cow: Money maker.
CER: Center for Education Reform.
character education: Intentional development of ethics and values.
charter: Contract between school and authorizer to form a charter school.
charter management organization (CMO): Nonprofit organization that offers charter management services.
charter school: Charter schools are nonsectarian public schools of choice that operate with freedom from many of the regulations that apply to traditional public schools.
charter school cap: Legal limit of number of charter schools and/or students enrolled.
charter school law: Legislation to permit charter schools and how they may operate.
charter school litmus test: There is none.
charter school organization: Organized group that supports charter schools by providing information, resources, and much more.
charter school supporter: Person who supports charter schools.
charter school tuition: There is none.
cherry-picking: Picking the best.
classical education: Form of education based on traditions from Western culture.

college prep: Preparation for college-bound students.
communications folder: Folder containing homework, newsletters, and/or other material exchanged between school and home.
community service: Certainnumber of hours that may be required of students/families to participate in activities, which benefit the institute or community.
conduct violation: Breach in behavior expectations.
conversion charter school: Charter school that replaces a closed traditional school.
core knowledge: Popular curriculum based on E.D. Hirsch's writings.
creaming: Attracting the best.
Curriculum: Course of study.
Department of Education: The U.S. government agency that ensures equal access to education and promotes fair education excellence.
director: CEO of the charter school.
dress code: Definitions of proper attire.
dress code violation: Inappropriate attire.
early college: College course during K-12 studies.
"Education by Charter": Document by Ray Budde that started charter school movement.
Education Management Organization: For-profit business that offers charter management services.
employee enrollment policy: Rules pertaining to enrolling children of school employees.
enrollment: Registration.
entrepreneurship: Practice of starting a new organization.
ESL: English as Second Language.
expeditionary learning: Project-based learning with roots in Outward Bound.
extended school year: School year that goes beyond traditional scheduling and sometimes includes mandatory summer school.
extracurricular activities: Activities pertinent to students, but may not apply to regular classroom learning.
federally subsidized lunch: Lunch funded by federal moneys.
first-come-first-served enrollment: School registration according to date of application.
for-profit: A business legally recognized as an organization that sells goods or services to consumers and reports a profit.
founder: Someone who establishes an organization.

funding: Financing.
governing council: operating board.
grant: monetary aid, or permission.
grassroots network: Involvement of common citizens organizing locally.
grievance policy: Proper and effective filing and management of complaints and feedback.
GT: gifted and talented.
handpicking: Selecting the best.
highly qualified teacher: Teachers qualified to teach according to the No Child Left Behind standards.
Homeschool: Home-based learning.
homework: Schoolwork to be completed after class.
International Baccalaureate: Demanding preuniversity program that allows students to earn college credits.
K-12: Kindergarten through 12th grade education.
Letter of Commitment: A letter that formalizes the recognition of responsibilities between school and home.
letter of intent: A form that states the intent to enroll.
lottery enrollment: School admission based on random drawing.
Mission: Goal.
mom-and-pop charter school: Charter school started by parents.
money tree: If you have one, please mail it to your nearest charter school organization.
Montessori: Maria Montessori: Italian educator who developed the Montessori teaching method.
NAPCS: National Association for Public Charter Schools.
NCLB: No Child Left Behind.
networking: Building relationships with individuals and organizations who share causes or goals.
No Child Left Behind: A law passed in 2002 in which the overall purpose of the law is to ensure that each child in America is able to meet high learning standards.
nonprofit: an organization that does not distribute its surplus funds to owners or shareholders, but instead uses them to further its goals.
online: Connected to a computer network.
open classroom: Student-centered learning.
open enrollment: Period of time when enrollment applications are accepted.
open house: Scheduled availability for visiting and viewing.

operating council: governing board.
outreach: Effort of connecting with the general public.
parent union: Organized parent representation.
parental involvement: Two-way meaningful communication/participation between parents and education institute.
parent-teacher conference: Scheduled meeting between teacher and parent to discuss student progress.
permanent building: The facility that hosts the school long-term.
PPR: Per Pupil Revenue.
principal: Director, head of school.
private school: School funded by endowment or tuition, operated by private entity.
project-based learning: Use of classroom projects to teach students.
PTA: Parent Teacher Association (also known as Parent Teacher Organization PTO).
public school: Tax-paid education with control and funding coming from three levels: federal, state, and local.
SAC: School Accountability Committee.
school bus: Bus transportation specifically designated for schools.
school choice: Choosing a school when there are options.
school closure: A school that is closed due to varying circumstances.
school district: Geographic entities in a state or county, or local officials provide public educational services for the area's residents.
school facility: School building.
school uniform: Designated schoolwear.
scope: The sum of deliverables to be provided by the project (school).
seeding: Deliberately seeking quality charter schools for a district or location.
sibling enrollment policy: Rules regarding how siblings of enrolled students may be admitted to a school.
SPED: Special Education.
staff: Hired employees.
standardized test: Testing that is administered and scored in a consistent manner (e.g., state standardized tests).
STEM: Science, Technology, Engineering, and Math.
structured: May refer to set programming, scheduling, or expectations.
student: Child who is enrolled at a school.
study groups: Group of students who meet to study.
teachers union: Organized teacher representation.

teamwork: Coordinated effort.

temporary building: Facility that may temporarily house a school until a long-term building is available.

traditional public schools: Neighborhood schools, district-run schools.

tutor: Specialized education coach.

volunteer hours: Number of hours of personal time donated to the school or cause.

volunteerism: Willingness of people to contribute to a cause without personal financial gain.

vote: A formalized expression of choice or preference.

waiting list: List of individuals who were not able to enroll because quantity of interested individuals outnumbered availability.

Helpful links

The Center for Education Reform
www.edreform.com

The Independence Institute
www.i2i.org

National Alliance for Public Charter Schools
www.publiccharters.org

National Charter School Institute
www.nationalcharterschools.org

School Choice for Kids
www.schoolchoiceforkids.org

United States Department of Education
www.ed.gov/parents

US Charter Schools
www.uscharterschools.org

Charter School Organizations

Alaska Department of Education
801 West 10th Street, Suite 200
P.O. Box 110500
Juneau, AK 99811-0500
Phone: 907-465-2800
www.alaska.gov

Algiers Charter Schools Association
3712 MacArthur Suite 100A
New Orleans, 70014
Phone: 504-302-7000
www.algierscharterschools.org

American Academy for Liberal Education (AALE) Charter School Initiative
1050 17th Street NW, Suite 400
Washington, DC 20036
Phone: 202-452-8611
www.aale.org

Arizona Charter Schools Association
7500 N. Dreamy Draw Drive, Suite 220
Phoenix, AZ 85020
Phone: 602-944-0644
www.azcharters.org

Arizona State Board for Charter Schools
1700 W. Washington Street
Room 164
Phoenix, AZ 85007
Phone: 602-364-3080
www.asbcs.az.gov

Arkansas Public School Resource Center
1401 West Capitol , Suite 465
Little Rock, AR 72201
Phone: 501-492-4300
www.apsrc.net

Arkansas Department of Education
Four Capitol Mall, Room 105-C
Little Rock, AR 72201
Phone: 501-683-5313
www.arkansased.org/schools/schools_charter.html

Association Charter Educators (ACE) of Texas
3800 Main Street, Suite E
Dallas, TX 78768
Phone: 214-914-9664
www.aceoftexas.org

Building Excellent Schools
262 Washington Street, 7th Floor
Boston, MA 02108
Phone: (617) 227-4545
www.buildingexcellentschools.org

California Charter Schools Association
250 E. 1st Street, Suite 1000
Los Angeles, CA 90012
Phone: 213-244-1446
www.charterassociation.org

California Department of Education-Charter Schools Office
School Fiscal Services Division
1430 N Street, Room 3800
Sacramento, CA 95814-5901
Phone: 916-319-0800
www.cde.ca.gov

Center for School Change
University of Minnesota.
301 19th Avenue South, Rm. 234
Minneapolis, MN 55455
Phone: 612-626-1834
www.centerforschoolchange.org

Charter School Association of Indiana
Organization is in transition. No contact information available at this time
Charter Schools Development Center
7750 College Town Drive, Suite 100
Sacramento, CA 95826
Phone: 916-278-6069
www.chartercenter.org

Charter Schools Institute
State University of New York
41 State St., Suite 700
Albany, NY 12207
Phone: 518-433-8277
www.newyorkcharters.org

Charter School Policy Institute-Next Step for Texas
805 West 10th Street, Suite 302
Austin, TX 78701
Phone: 512-371-8888
www.charterschoolpolicy.org

Charter School Resource Center of Tennessee
511 Union Street, Suite 740
Nashville, TN 37219
Phone: 615-248-6401

Colorado Department of Education
201 E. Colfax Ave
Denver, CO 80203
Phone: 303-866-6600
www.cde.state.co.us

Colorado League of Charter Schools
725 S. Broadway, Suite 7
Denver, CO 80209
Phone: 303-989-5356
www.coloradoleague.org

Connecticut Coalition for Achievement Now **(ConnCAN)**
85 Willow Street
New Haven, CT 06511
Phone: 203-772-4017
www.conncan.org

Connecticut State Department of Education
165 Capitol Avenue
Hartford, CT 06106
Phone: 860-713-6543
www.sde.ct.gov

D.C. Association of Chartered Public Schools
910 17th Street, NW
Suite 1150
Washington, DC 20006
Phone: 202-296-7205
www.dcpcsa.org

Delaware Charter Schools Network
100 West 10th Street, Suite 403
Wilmington, DE 19801
Phone: (302) 778-5999
www.decharternetwork.org

Delaware Department of Education
John G. Townsend Building
401 Federal Street
Dover, DE 19901
Phone: 302-735-4000
www.doe.k12.de.us

Families for Excellence in Education
11016 Quail Creek Road
Oklahoma City, OK 73120
Phone: 405-755-9014
www.familiesforexcellence.com

Florida Charter School Resource Center
University of South Florida
4202 East Fowler Avenue
HMS 401
Tampa, FL 33620
Phone: 813-974-3858
www.icoedu.usf.edu

Florida Consortium of Public Charter Schools
1126 South Federal Highway, Suite 170
Fort Lauderdale, Florida 33316
Phone: 954-463-9595
www.floridacharterschools.org

Friends of Choice in Urban Schools (FOCUS)
1530 16th Street, NW, Suite 104
Washington, DC 20036
Phone: 202-387-0405
www.focusdc.org

Georgia Charter Schools Association, Inc.
600 West Peachtree Street NW, Suite 1555
Atlanta, GA 30308
Phone: 404-460-9992
www.gacharters.org

Georgia Department of Education
2054 Twin Towers East
205 Jesse Hill Jr. Drive SE
Atlanta, GA 30334
Phone: 404-656-2800
www.doe.k12.ga.us

Greater Educational Opportunities Foundation
2540 N. Capitol Avenue, Suite 101
Indianapolis, IN 46208
Phone: 317-536-1027
www.geofoundation.org

Hawaii Charter Schools Administrative Office
1111 Bishop Street
Suite 516
Honolulu, HI 96813
Phone: 808-586-3775
www.hcsao.org

Idaho Charter School Network (ICSN), Boise State University College of Education
1910 University Drive, MS 1745
Room, 415
Boise, ID 83725
Phone: 208-426-1837
www.csi.boisestate.edu/icsn.htm

Idaho Department of Education
650 West State Street
P.O. Box 83720
Boise, ID 83720-0027
Phone: 208-332-6800
www.sde.idaho.gov

Illinois Network of Charter Schools
205 West Randolph Street
Chicago, IL 60604
Phone: 312-235-0798
www.incschools.org

Illinois State Board of Education
100 N. 1st Street
Springfield, IL 62777
Phone: 866-262-6663
www.isbe.net

Indiana Department of Education
151 West Ohio Street
Indianapolis, IN 46204
Phone: 317-232-6610
www.doe.state.in.us

Indiana Public Charter Schools Association
407 Fulton Street, Suite 301
Indianapolis, IN 46202
Phone: 317-972-5880
www.incharters.org

Iowa Department of Education (IA DOE)
Grimes State Office Building
Des Moines, IA 50319
Phone: 515-281-8402
www.iowa.gov/educate

Kansas Department of Education
120 SE 10th Avenue
Topeka, KS 66612-1182
Phone: 785-296- 3201
www.ksde.org

The League of Charter Schools
200 Stags Trail
Suite 306
Chapel Hill, NC 27516
Phone: (919) 967-1029
www.charterleague.org

Louisiana Charter School Association
5500 Prytania Street #126
New Orleans, LA 70115
Phone: 504-274-3651
Contact: Caroline Roemer
www.lacharterschools.org

Louisiana Department of Education
1201 North Third St.
P.O. Box 94064
Capitol Station
Baton Rouge, LA 70804-9064
Phone: 877-453-2721
www.doe.state.la.us

Maryland Charter School Network
P.O. Box 1033
Baltimore, MD 21203
Phone: 800-689-3795
www.mdcharternetwork.org

Maryland State Department of Education
200 W. Baltimore Street
Baltimore, MD 21201-2595
Phone: 410-767- 0600
www.msde.state.md.us

Massachusetts Charter Public School Association
10 Tremont Street, 6th Floor
Boston, MA 02108
Phone: (617) 523-0881
www.masscharterschools.org

Massachusetts Department of Education
75 Pleasant Street
Malden, MA 02148-9406
Phone: 781-338-3000
www.doe.mass.edu

Michigan Association of Public School Academies (MAPSA)
215 South Washington Square, Suite 135, Suite 210
Lansing, MI 48933
Phone: 517-374-9167
www.charterschools.org

Michigan Department of Education
608 W. Allegan Street
P.O. Box 30008
Lansing, MI 48909
Phone: 517-373- 3324
www.michigan.gov

Minnesota Association of Charter Schools (MACS)
351 E. Kellogg Blvd.
St. Paul, MN 55101
Phone: 651-789-3090
www.mncharterschools.org

Minnesota Department of Children, Families and Learning
1500 Highway 36 W
Roseville, MN 55113
Phone: 651-582-8200
www.state.mn.us

Mississippi Center for Public Policy
P.O. Box 13514
Jackson, MS 39236
Phone: 601-969-1300
www.mspolicy.org

Mississippi Department of Education
P.O. Box 771
359 North West Street
Jackson, MS 39201
Phone: 601-359- 3513
www.mde.k12.ms.us

Missouri Department of Elementary and Secondary Education
P.O. Box 480
Jefferson City, MO 65102
Phone: 573-751- 4212
www.dese.mo.gov

The National Alliance of Public Charter Schools
1101 Fifteenth Street, NW, Suite 1010
Washington, DC 20005
Phone: 202-289-2700
www.publiccharters.org

National Association of Charter School Authorizers
105 W. Adams Street, Suite 1430
Chicago, IL 60603-6253
Phone: 312-376-2300
Fax: 312-376-2400
www.qualitycharters.org

National Charter Schools Institute
2520 S. University Park Drive, Suite Box 11
Mount Pleasant, MI 48858
Phone: 989-774-2999
www.nationalcharterschools.org

Nevada Department of Education
700 East Fifth Street
Carson City, NV 89701-5096
Phone: 775-687-9200
www.doe.nv.gov

Nevada Public Charter Schools
P.O. Box 50128
Aparks, NV 89435
Phone: 775-626-4619
www.nvpubliccharterschools.org

New Hampshire Center for School Reform
P.O. Box 2464
Concord, NH 03301
Phone: 603-224-0366
www.nhschoolreform.org

New Hampshire Department of Education
101 Pleasant Street
Concord, NH 03301-3860
Phone: 603-271-3494
www.ed.state.nh.us

New Jersey Charter Public Schools Association
349 West State Street, 4th Floor
Trenton, NJ 08618
Phone: 609-989-9700
www.njcharters.org

New Jersey Charter School Resource Center
Center for Effective School Practices, Rutgers
80 Cottontail Lane, Suite 410
Somerset, NJ 08873
Phone: 732-564-9087
www.rci.rutgers.edu

New Jersey Department of Education (NJ DOE)
P.O. Box 500
Trenton, NJ 08625-0500
Phone: 609-292-4469
www.state.nj.us

New Mexico Coalition for Charter Schools
610 Gold Avenue SW, Suite 224
Albuquerque, NM 87102
Phone: 505-842-8203
www.nmccs.org

New Mexico Public Education Department
300 Don Gaspar
Santa Fe, NM 87501-2786
Phone: 505-827- 5800
www.ped.state.nm.us

New York Charter Schools Association
120 Broadway
Albany, NY 12204
Phone: 518-694-3110
www.nycsa.org

New York Charter School Resource Center
1 Penn Plaza
36th Floor
250 West 34th Street
New York, NY 10119
Phone: 888-343-6907
www.nycsrc.org

New York City Center for Charter School Excellence
111 Broadway
Suite 604
New York, NY 10006
Phone: 212-437-8300
www.nycchartercenter.org

New York State Education Department
89 Washington Avenue
Room 462 EBA
Albany, NY 12234
Phone: 518-474-3852
www.nysed.gov

North Carolina Department of Education
301 N. Wilmington Street
Raleigh, NC 27601
Phone: 919-807-3300
www.dpi.state.nc.us

Office of Independent Education and Parental Choice
Florida Department of Education
325 West Gaines Street, Suite 522
Tallahassee, FL 32399
Phone: 800-447-1636
www.fldoe.org

Ohio Alliance for Public Charter Schools (OAPCS)
33 N. Third Street, Suite 600
Columbus, 43215
Phone: 614-744-2266
www.oapcs.org

Ohio Department of Education
25 S. Front Street
Columbus, OH 43215-4183
Phone: 614-995-1129
www.ode.state.oh.us

Oklahoma Charter School Association
12600 N. Kelley Avenue
Oklahoma City, OK 73131
Phone: 405-409-2860

Oklahoma Department of Education
2500 North Lincoln Blvd.
Oklahoma City, OK 73105-4599
Phone: 405-521-3301
www.sde.state.ok.us

Oregon Center for Charter School Development
P.O. Box 50128
Sparks, NV 89435
Phone: 775-626-4691

Oregon Charter School Service Center
171 NE 102nd Avenue
Suite 302
Portland, OR 97220
Phone: 503-244-7523
www.oregoneducation.org

Oregon Department of Education
255 Capitol Street NE
Salem, OR 97310-0203
Phone: 503-947- 5600
www.oregon.gov

Oregon Department of Education Curriculum, Instruction and Field Service
255 Capitol Street NE
Salem, OR 97310-0203
Phone: 503-378-3600
www.oregon.gov

Pennsylvania Charter School Resource Center
2 Penn Center
Suite 1100
Philadelphia, PA 19102
Phone: 215-557-9919

Pennsylvania Coalition of Charter Schools
999 West Chester Pike, Suite B-6
West Chester, PA 19382
Phone: 877-572-9689
www.pachartercoalition.com

Pennsylvania Department of Education
333 Market Street
Harrisburg, PA 17126-0333
Phone: 717-783-3755
www.state.pa.us

Rhode Island Department of Education
255 Westminster Street
Providence, RI 02903-3400
Phone: 401-222-4600
www.ride.ri.gov

Rhode Island League of Charter Schools
4 Richmond Square, Suite 300
Providence, RI 02906
Phone: 401-831-3700 ext. 102
www.richarterschools.com

South Carolina Department of Education
1429 Senate Street, Suite 605
Columbia, SC 29201
Phone: 803-734-8500
www.sde.state.sc.us

Tennessee Charter Schools Association
3-22 Vanderbuilt Place
Nashville, 37172
Phone: 800-998-3349
www.tncharterschools.org

Tennessee Department of Education
710 James Robertson Pkwy.
Andrew Johnson Tower, 6th Floor
Nashville, TN 37243-0375
Phone: 615-741-2731
www.state.tn.us

Texas Charter Schools Association
700 Lavaca Street
Suite 930
Austin, Texas 78701
Phone: 512.584.TCSA (8272)
www.txcharterschools.org

Texas Education Agency (TEA)
1701 North Congress Avenue
Austin, TX 78701
Phone: 512-463-9734
www.tea.state.tx.us

University of Hawaii Charter School Resource Center
200 W. Kawili Street
Hilo, HI 96720
Phone: 808-974-7414
www.hawaii.edu

U.S. Department of Education (US DOE)
400 Maryland Avenue, SW
FOB-6, Room 3E116
Washington, DC 20202
Phone: 202-401-0113
www.ed.gov

Utah Association of Public Charter Schools
P.O. Box 58201
Salt Lake City, UT 84158
Phone: 801-953-2748
www.utahcharters.org

Utah Charter Schools Association
2416 East 1700 S.
Salt Lake City, UT 84108
Phone: 801-722-8911
www.utahcharterschools.org

Utah State Office of Education
250 East 500 South
Salt Lake City, UT 84114
Phone: 801-538-7740
www.schools.utah.gov

Virginia Charter School Resource Center
1600 Wilson Blvd., Suite 900
Arlington, VA 22209
Phone: 703-522-5809
www.virginiacharterschools.org

Virginia Department of Education
P.O. Box 2120
James Monroe Building
101 N. 14th Street
Richmond, VA 23218-2120
Phone: 804-292-3820
www.doe.virginia.gov

Wisconsin Charter Schools Association
P.O. Box 1704
Madison, WI 53701-1704
Phone: 608- 261-1120
www.wicharterschools.org

Wisconsin Department of Public Instruction
125 S. Webster Street
Madison, WI 53707-7841
Phone: 800-441-4563
www.dpi.wi.gov

Wyoming Department of Education
2020 Grand Avenue
Suite 500
Laramie, WY 82070
Phone: 307-777-5296
www.k12.wy.us

Award-Winning Charter Schools Index

There are more than 4,500 charter schools in the United States. Due to limited space we regrettably could not list all schools here. Please contact your state education department or charter school organization for additional information about charter schools near you. The following charter schools were recently recognized for excellence through *Newsweek* or *U.S. News* top schools awards, and the National Charter School of the Year Award through the Center for Education Reform:

Academic Center of Excellence, Cabot, AR
web.mac.com/cabotace/iWeb/ACE/Homepage.html

Academy at the Farm, Dade City, FL
www.academyatthefarm.com

Amber Charter School, New York, NY
ambercharter.echalk.com

American Indian Public Charter School, Oakland, CA
www.aipcs.org

Animo Leadership Charter High School, Inglewood, CA
www.greendot.org/leadership

Ann Arbor Learning Community, Ann Arbor, MI
www.annarborlearningcommunity.org

Basis Tucson, Tucson, AZ
www.basistucson.org

Bear Creek Community Charter School, Wilkes Barre, PA
www.bearcreekschool.com

Benjamin Franklin Senior High School, New Orleans, LA
www.benfranklinhighschool.org

Challenge Charter School, Glendale, AZ
www.challengecharterschool.net

Chamblee Charter High School, Chamblee, GA
www.dekalb.k12.ga.us/chambleehs

The Charter School of Wilmington, Wilmington, DE
www.charterschool.org

Coeur d'Alene, ID
www.cdacharter.org

Community of Peace Academy, St. Paul, MN
www.cpa.charter.k12.mn.us

Cornerstone Academy, Houston, TX
csa.springbranchisd.com

Detroit Edison Public School Academy, Detroit, MI
www.detroitedisonpsa.org

Discovery School, Lancaster, SC
dis.lancasterscschools.org

Dolores Huerta Preparatory HS, Pueblo, Colorado
www.cca-pueblo.org

Excel Academy Charter School, East Boston, MA
www.excelacademy.org

Explore Charter School, Brooklyn, NY
www.explorecharterschool.org

The Fort Worth Academy of Fine Arts, Fort Worth, TX
www.fwafa.org

Gaston College Preparatory, Gaston, NC
www.kippnorthcarolina.org

Greenville Technical Charter High School, Greenville, SC
www.gtchs.org

Guajome Park Academy, Vista, CA
www.guajome.net

Harlem Village Academies New York, NY
www.villageacademies.org

Hawthorne Math & Science Academy High, Hawthorne, CA
www.hawthornemsa.org

Hoboken Charter School, Hoboken, NJ
www.hobokencs.org

Idea College Preparatory, Donna, TX
www.ideapublicschools.org

Independence Charter School, Philadelphia, PA
www.independencecharter.org

The International School of Louisiana, New Orleans, LA
www.isl-edu.org

Jefferson Academy Elementary, Broomfield, CO
www.jajags.com

John Greenleaf Whittier School, Milwaukee, WI
www2.milwaukee.k12.wi.us/whittier

Kennesaw Charter School, Kennesaw, GA
www.kennesawcharter.com

Kinston Charter Academy, Kinston, NC
www.kinstoncharteracademy.com

KIPP San Francisco Bay Academy, San Francisco, CA
www.sfbayacademy.org

The Laboratory Charter School of Commun. & Lang., Bala Cynwyd, PA
www.labcharter.org

Lennox Academy Mathematics Science and Technology, Lennox, CA
lmsta.lennox.k12.ca.us

Liberty Common School, Ft. Collins, CO
www.libertycommon.org

Lisa Academy, Little Rock, AR
www.lisaacademy.org

MATCH Charter Public School, Boston, MA
www.matchschool.org

Mathematics Science & Technology Community Charter, Philadelphia, PA
www.mastcharter.org

Midland Valley Preparatory School, Graniteville, SC
No Web site

Moreno Valley High School, Angel Fire, NM
www.mvhsnm.org

Northland Preparatory Academy, Flagstaff, AZ
www.northlandprep.org

Oscar De La Hoya Animo Charter High School, Los Angeles, CA
www.greendot.org/delahoya

Pacific Collegiate Charter, Santa Cruz, CA
www.pacificcollegiate.com

Paul Cuffee School, Providence, RI
www.paulcuffee.org

Peak to Peak Charter School, Lafayette, CO
www.peaktopeak.org

Pembroke Pines Charter Schools, Pembroke Pines, FL
www.pinescharter.com

Prairie Crossing Charter School, Grayslake, IL
www.pccs.lake.k12.il.us

Preuss School UCSD, La Jolla, CA
preuss.ucsd.edu

Princeton Charter School, Princeton, NJ
www.pcs.k12.nj.us

Raleigh Charter High School, Raleigh, NC
www.raleighcharterhs.org

Renaissance Academy, Phoenixville, PA
www.rak12.org

Ridgeview Classical School, Fort Collins, CO
www.ridgeviewclassical.com

Roxbury Preparatory Charter School, Roxbury, MA
www.roxburyprep.org

Signature School, Evansville, IN
www.signature.edu

Star Charter School, Austin, TX
www.starcharterschool.org

Sturgis Charter Public School, Hyannis, MA
www.sturgischarterschool.com

Synergy Charter Academy, Los Angeles, CA
http://wearesynergy.org

Taos Municipal Charter School, Taos, NM
www.taoscharterschool.org

Toledo School for the Arts, Toledo, OH
www.ts4arts.org

Triumphant Learning Center, Safford, AZ
myweb.cableone.net/tlctiger

21st Century Public Academy, Albuquerque, NM
www.21stcenturypa.org

University High School, Fresno, CA
www.csufresno.edu/univhigh

Western Village Academy, Oklahoma City, OK
www.wvacademy.com

Yes Prep Public Schools, Houston, TX
www.yesprep.org

INDEX

A

academic strengths, 31
accelerated math options, 33
accountability, 182–184, 216, 217
administrative staff, 46–47
administrative support, volunteer, 147
administrators, 38–40
admissions, school, 140–143
advocacy, 160–166, 189–191
agreements, sample school, 76–78, 79–82
alcohol abuse programs, 101
all-charter districts, 29
American Academy (CO), 89
American Federation of Teachers, 28
application, enrollment, 140–143
Asperger's syndrome, 103–105
ASPIRE Public schools, 41
"at risk" students
    cases, 108–109
    defining, 100–101
    gifted students, 107
    online learning for, 128
    parents, 148
    schools designed for, 18, 52
athletic programs, 117
authorizers, charter school, 169–178, 182–183, 186
autistic children, 100
autonomy of schools, 188

B

benefits of charter schools, 193–194
Benigno, Pam, 189
blended online/classroom schools, 128–129
blogging, 164–165
boards, district school, 170
boards, governing, 37–38, 148, 163, 182–183

Budde, Ray, 28–29
budget management, 39, 46, 146, 181
buildings, school, 20–22, 116–119, 180
buses, school, 120
business community involvement, 73–74
business skills, 39
business-focused schools, 90–91

C

cap on number of schools, 203–304
caring culture, 31
carpooling, 67–68, 120–121
Center for Education Reform (CER), 162, 187, 189, 216–217
certification of teachers, 47
character development, 92–94, 109
charter application and renewal, 176–177
charter management organizations (CMO), 37, 41–42, 169, 213–214
charter schools
    benefits of, 193–194
    community involvement, 73–74
    defined, 23, 26
    funding of, 23, 179–180, 188, 202, 217
    networking together, 160–162, 189
    public perception of, 72, 200–205
    starting, 206–213
    success of, 222–223
cherry-picking (myth), 201–202
child learning styles, 130–132
choice vs. competition, 20–22
choosing schools, 16–18, 19, 124–125
The Classical Academy (CO), 62–63, 79–82, 88

classical education schools, 87–88
classroom sizes, 51, 54
Cleveland Entrepreneurship Preparatory School, 90–91
Clinton, Bill, 29
closures of charter schools, 177–178, 215, 216–221
   preventing, 220–221
college prep-focused schools, 86–87
Colorado High School Charter, 55–56, 59–60
commitments, 76–78
committees, school, 147
communication, parent-teacher, 152–156
community involvement, 73–74
Community of Peace Academy (MN), 109–110
community service, student, 73, 149
comparing schools, 132–140
compassion, 62–63
competition vs. choice, 20–22
contract districts, 29
Core Knowledge programs, 32, 83–84
cost management, 46
councils, governing, 37–38, 148, 163, 182–183
Cousins, Emily, 84
creaming (myth), 200–201
credo, shool, 93
curricula types. *see* school curricula types

D

deans, 38–40
demographics, racial, 203
Denver Public Schools, 20–22
Denver School of Science and Technology, 118
Denver Venture School, 73–74
directors, school, 38–40
discipline codes, 51, 112–113
districts, school, 29, 171
diversity of students, 17, 58
draining funds (myth), 202
dress codes, 68, 114–115
dual enrollment early college, 86
dyslexia, 110

E

early college programs, 86–87
"Education by Charter", 28–29
education management organizations (EMO), 37, 42–44
education quality, 18–19
elections, public office, 163–164, 165, 189
employee children enrollment, 143
engineering-focused schools, 88–89
English as a Second Language (ESL), 101–102, 109–110
enrollment policies, 200–202
enrollment process, 140–143
entrepreneurial charter schools, 41, 43, 168–169
entrepreneurship focus, 90–91
Envision Schools, 41
ethics, educating, 92–94
evaluating a child's learning style, 130–132
evaluating schools, 132–140
events, special, 147
executives of schools, 38–40
expectations of students, 77–78
Expeditionary Learning curricula, 84–85

F

facilities, school, 20–22, 116–119, 180
factors in choosing a school, 124
fees, 143–144
finances, 204–205, 217
foreign languages, 102
for-profit management companies, 42–44
founding, charter school, 168–169, 206–213

franchise-type schools, 42, 169
funding, 23, 179–180, 188, 202, 217

G

Gertz-Ressler High School (CA), 166
gifted and talented
  schools, 107–108
  students, 18, 58, 98
governing boards, 32, 37–38, 148, 163, 182–183
grant funding, 180
grassroots networks, 165
Green Dot Public Schools (CA), 195
grooming, 114–115
guest speakers, classroom, 147
guide, school comparison, 132–139

H

Hahn, Kurt, 84
heads of schools, 38–40
higher education authorizers, 170
hired management organizations, 41–44
Hirsch, E.D., 83
history of charter schools, 28–29
homework, 95–97
Hope Online Learning Academy Co-Op (CO), 108–109
  educator testimonial, 52–53
  founding of, 211–212
  hybrid online/classroom instruction, 129
  student cases, 63–64
human aspect of education, 31
hybrid online/classroom schools, 128–129

I

IDEA College Preparatory Donna (TX), 60–61
immigrant students, 109–110
Indianapolis Charter Schools Initiative, 171–174, 220
individual education plan (IEP), 60, 104, 110
individualism, student, 30–31
Infinity Charter School (PA), 107
innovation in education, 17–18, 169, 182, 188, 193–195
interscholastic sports, 117
involvement, parent, 146–150

J

James Irwin Charter Elementary School (CO), 34

K

Knowledge is Power Program (KIPP) schools
  directors, criteria for, 39–40
  school foundings, 169
  teacher, parent, and student commitments, 76–78
  teacher availability to parents, 69
  type of school, 41

L

languages, foreign, 102
laws, federal, 186–187
laws, state, 187–191
leadership skills, 39–40
learning styles, child, 130–132
lobbying, 189–191
local school boards, 170
lottery admission, 142
lunch program, 118

M

management organizations, hired, 41–44
math, accelerated options, 33
math and science-focused schools, 88–89
mayoral authority, 170, 171
Media and Technology Charter

High School (MATCH) (MA), 118–119
members, governing board, 37
Michigan Council of Charter School Authorizers, 219–220
Minnesota, 29, 187
misconduct, 112–113
Montesorri programs, 56–57, 85
morals, educating, 92–94
myths, 200–205

N

National Alliance for Public Charter Schools, 162
National School of Character, 109
Network for Teaching Entrepreneurship, 91
networking among charter schools, 160–162, 189
New York Center for Autism Charter School, 100
New York public schools, 22
New York State Board of Regents, 172–174
No Child Left Behind (NCLB), 186
North Star Academy (CO), 103–105
not-for-profit management organizations, 41–42

O

online schools, 128
online/classroom hybrid schools, 128–129, 211–212
Ooms, Alexander, 20–22
open classroom schools, 127
open enrollment, 143
operating councils (governing boards), 37–38, 148, 163, 182–183
organizations, charter school, 162
Our World Neighborhood Foundation, 93–94
outsourcing management, 41
Outward Bound USA, 84
oversight, administrative, 183–184

P

Paideia curriculum schools, 87–88
Parent Revolution (organization), 166
parent testimonials, 30–34
parents
    carpooling, 67–68
    characteristics, 65–67
    choosing schools, 20–22
    commitments, 77
    determination of, 67
    as researchers, 66
    as school founders, 168–169
    unions, 165–166
    volunteering. see volunteering, parent
parent-student relationship, 156–159
parent-teacher relationships, 50–51, 69–70, 151–156
Parker Core Knowledge Charter School (CO), 53–55
per pupil revenue, 179
philanthropists, 204–205
pillars of character, 93
Platte River Academy (CO), 110–111
political issues, 160, 163, 192–198
Polk County School Board (FL), 171, 174–175, 177–178
Princeton House Charter School (FL), 100
public perception of charter schools, 72
punishments, 112–113

Q

questionnaires, school comparison, 132–139

R

racial demographics, 203
research guide, 130–133
researching schools, 132–140

resources, web site, 140, 162, 191
responsibility in students, 62–63
Ridgeview Classical School (CO), 60–61, 106
"at risk" students
    cases, 108–109
    defining, 100–101
    gifted students, 107
    online learning for, 128
    parents, 148
    schools designed for, 18, 52

S

school accountability committee (SAC), 183–184
school boards, local and state, 170
school committees, 147
school curricula types
    classical education, 87–88
    college prep/early college, 86–87
    Core Knowledge, 83–84
    entrepreneurship focus, 90–91
    Expeditionary Learning, 84–85
    Montesorri, 85
    STEM focus, 88–89
school instruction types, 127–129
    online/classroom hybrid, 128–129
    open classroom, 127
    traditional classroom, 127
school numbers, cap on, 203–304
school size, 188
science and technology programs, 88–89
self-governing, 32
self-paced learning, 56, 64
sequenced learning, 83
Shanker, Albert, 28, 29, 195
sibling preference enrollment, 143
size of schools, 188
Socratic method, 80, 81, 88
special education (SPED), 98–101
    students, 104–106, 110–111
sports programs, 117
staff, school, 46–47
standardized tests, 24
starting a charter school, 206–213
    advice, 209–214
    funding, 208
    networking, 206, 208
    political issues, 208–209
    researching, 206–207
    timing, 209
state laws, 187–191
STEM-focused schools, 88–89
student learning styles, 130–132
students
    commitments, 78, 149
    diversity of, 58
    teacher relationship, 156–159
    testimonials, 59–63
student-teacher-parent relationships, 151–152
substance abuse programs, 101
success of charter schools, 222–223
SUNY Charter Schools Institute (NY), 172–174
support for charter schools, 160–162

T

teacher-initiated schools, 28
teachers, 45, 47–57
    choosing to work at charter schools, 50–55
    commitments, 76
    parent relationships with, 50–51, 69–70, 151–156
    qualifications, 24, 47–49
    salaries, 49–50
    student relationships with, 156–159
    unions, 194–196
teamwork, educational, 151–152
testimonials, parent, 30–34
testimonials, teacher, 52–55
testing, standardized, 24
time requirements, homework, 96
Toledo School of the Arts, 30–31
Tore, Joseph A., 30–31

traditional classroom schools, 127
transportation, 67–68, 120–121
Trillium Academy (MI), 56–57
trivium educational approach, 87–88
tuition, 17, 23

U

understanding, letters of, 79–82
uniforms, 68–69, 114–115
unions, parent, 165–166
unions, teacher, 28, 29, 50, 194–196
uniqueness, 18, 26–27
United Federation of Teachers (UFT), 195
University Academy Charter High School (NJ), 119
university authorizers, 170
U.S. Department of Education, 186

V

Vaughn Next Century Learning Center Charter School (CA), 179
virtues, educating, 92–94
volunteering, parent, 70, 146–150
    financial need for, 146, 180
    online, 128
    requirement, 47, 146, 148
    types of, 47, 147–148
volunteering, student, 149
voting, 165, 189

W

waiting lists, 142–143
Washington Latin Public Charter School (DC), 94
web site resources, 140, 162, 191
Windermere Park Charter Academy, 33
working parents, 148
worksheets, school comparison, 132–139

Y

YES Prep Public Schools (TX), 86–87

CPSIA information can be obtained at www.ICGtesting.com
Printed in the USA
LVOW12s0901111113

360814LV00015B/443/P